ENJOY!

[signature]

For more than three decades, I have spoken thousands of times to churches across the country about biblical financial stewardship principles. I have also counseled tens of thousands, if not hundreds of thousands, of individuals across the country about how to be good stewards of the resources that they have been given. As a result, I have come to learn that most people don't know much about money, especially when it comes to how to invest properly for retirement.

As Anthony clearly delineates, there is a significant difference as to how you should be invested in the accumulation phase of life compared to the distribution phase of life once you retire. You only get one shot at retirement, and it is the most expensive purchase that you will ever make so you cannot afford to make a mistake. If you want to do it right the first time, you must have a plan.

In the pages that follow, Anthony shares what you need to know to successfully develop that plan and sidestep the many potholes that lay ahead of you in retirement. Among other things, you will learn how to invest properly for the phase of life that you're in, when to file for Social Security, how to protect your loved ones in case of a long-term illness, and how to invest for the income you need in retirement without having to "spend down" your principal.

If you are in or near retirement, I recommend that you read this book.

James Rickard

Former Chairman of the Board for The Master's University (www.masters.edu) and founder of Stewardship Services Foundation in Newhall, California (www.ssfoundation.net)

As a three-time Emmy Award winner, I knew how to make money; I just didn't know what to do with it afterwards. In his book, Anthony emphasizes that what you don't know about retirement *can* hurt you. When I met Anthony and the Providence Financial team, I knew absolutely nothing about retirement.

Anthony has the heart of a teacher. By reading his book, you will learn what you need to know to be able to retire successfully. It's not what you *do* know that will hurt you; it's what you *don't* know. I would encourage you to read this book and get the knowledge you need to have peace of mind in retirement like I do.

Linda Henrikson

Three-time Emmy Award winner for costume design

We joined the Providence Financial team in 2006 because we were on the brink of retirement and couldn't afford to make any mistakes as my wife was going through a tough battle with cancer (which thankfully she won). Over the years,

Anthony has taught us the same principles that he outlines in his book. Because we have followed these principles, we are able to enjoy retirement knowing that the income we are getting from our investments will last as long as we do. If you are about to retire, you need to read this book to ensure that you don't make any critical mistakes.

Michael Aviles
Businessman

As a Los Angeles City firefighter, I underwent rigorous training because making one mistake may cause someone to lose their life. As I approached the end of my career, I realized that I had no training when it came to retirement planning. I also knew that a mistake may cost us our financial lives.

Over the last decade, Anthony has discussed many of the topics in his book with us. As I read it, it dawned on me that this book is a training manual for retirement. You will learn what you need to know to retire with confidence so that you can sleep well at night.

Stephen Norris
Retired Los Angeles City Firefighter

Anthony has always believed that a financial plan is not complete without an estate plan. We signed up for our Living Trust with Anthony over a decade ago while attending a seminar that his firm was giving and it was through this that we became clients. In his book, Anthony dedicates an entire chapter to the discussion of estate planning. You will learn what you need to know to make sure that the assets you've worked hard for go to those whom you love instead of those whom the court chooses.

Bill and Charline Capps

More Life Than Money

More Life Than Money

HOW NOT TO OUTLIVE YOUR SAVINGS

Anthony A. Saccaro, ChFC, Esq.

 | Books

Published by Advantage, Charleston, South Carolina.
Member of Advantage Media Group.

ADVANTAGE is a registered trademark, and the Advantage colophon is a trademark of Advantage Media Group, Inc.

Printed in the United States of America.

10 9 8 7 6 5 4 3 2 1

ISBN: 978-1-64225-614-7 (Hardcover)
ISBN: 978-1-64225-613-0 (eBook)

LCCN: 2022914179

This publication is designed to provide accurate and authoritative information in regard to the subject matter covered. It is sold with the understanding that the publisher is not engaged in rendering legal, accounting, or other professional services. If legal advice or other expert assistance is required, the services of a competent professional person should be sought.

Advantage Media Group is a publisher of business, self-improvement, and professional development books and online learning. We help entrepreneurs, business leaders, and professionals share their Stories, Passion, and Knowledge to help others Learn & Grow. Do you have a manuscript or book idea that you would like us to consider for publishing? Please visit **advantagefamily.com**.

To my gorgeous wife, Anca, and my two beautiful kids, Aiden and Audria. You are the wind beneath my wings!

CONTENTS

DISCLAIMER

The information contained in this book is for educational purposes only and should not be considered as specific investment, financial, or legal advice, since I am not familiar with your situation. Should you have any questions about the contents within this book and whether any of the comments, suggestions, or recommendations apply to you, please consult with your financial advisor or attorney.

Providence Financial & Insurance Services Inc. is a registered investment advisory firm regulated by the Securities Exchange Commission CRD 141988. Anthony A. Saccaro is a life insurance agent in the state of California (license #0C62654).

FOREWORD

IN MY THIRTY-PLUS YEARS as a financial advisor, business owner, mentor, and coach, I've seen all sides of the financial services industry. However, I'm proud to say that Anthony Saccaro represents a lot of what's good in the industry.

In 2006, I founded Advisors' Academy with a vision to recruit other successful and like-minded advisors and teach them how to achieve even higher levels of success—while always keeping the interests of their clients first. Anthony has been an important part of Advisors' Academy, as a board member and member of the Advisors' Academy Founders Club. What started as mutual business respect for each other has evolved into a deep and abiding friendship. Anthony is the founder and president of Providence Financial & Insurance Services Inc. in Woodland Hills, California. One of the things I admire about Anthony is that when he decides to do something, he makes sure it's done the right way. Since estate planning is an essential component of a sound financial plan, Anthony wanted to make sure that he was able to offer this to his clients. In some states, a financial advisor is allowed to provide some estate planning services without being a licensed attorney, but not in California, where Anthony's practice is located. So Anthony took it upon himself to study to become an attorney in order to provide these services for his clients because of how important they are.

Anthony's focus on financial education is a great benefit to his clients. Like it says on the Providence Financial & Insurance Services website, "Smart and informed decisions can mean the difference between enjoying your golden years or struggling to make ends meet." I couldn't agree more.

It's true what Anthony writes as the title of chapter 1: "What You Don't Know Can Wreck Your Retirement." But it's also a big understatement. During my thirty-plus years in the retirement industry, I've noticed that it's what people are unaware of that ends up causing financial problems. That's why I'm so happy and proud that Anthony has taken the time to write this book. Anthony has been named to *Forbes* magazine's list of California's Financial Leaders, and his firm has also been on *Forbes'* list of Top Financial Planning Firms in California multiple times. He's written articles that have been featured in the *Wall Street Journal, USA Today, Barron's,* the *Los Angeles Daily News,* and many other publications. He's also been a guest on national financial news networks and shows such as Fox Business, CNBC, Yahoo Finance, and my national TV show, *The Income Generation.*

I can think of no one who is better qualified to educate and inform you about the risks and oversights that could derail your plans for retirement. I'm confident that by reading this book, you'll learn what you don't know so that you can make better-informed decisions about your financial future—so you can enjoy the retirement you've always envisioned.

David J. Scranton, CLU, ChFC, CFP®, CFA, MSFS

Founder of Advisors' Academy, Sound Income Strategies LLC, and the Retirement Income Store®

Host of the national TV show *The Income Generation*

Amazon best-selling author of *The Retirement Income Stor-E! The Story behind the Launch of The Retirement Income Store* (2019); and *Return on Principle: 7 Core Values to Help Protect Your Money in Good Times and Bad* (2016)

CHAPTER ONE

What You Don't Know Can Wreck Your Retirement

THE WHOLE GIST of this book is that there are things that you don't know about your retirement. And those things can really wreck your golden years. If you have listened to my radio show, heard me speak on TV or at a financial seminar, or watched the videos on my YouTube channel, you know I spend a lot of time talking about the fact that what you don't know can hurt you. I've been in practice for over two decades and have counseled thousands of retirees or folks who are close to retirement. I know a lot of stuff about money and how it works. Whatever your financial questions are, I'm pretty sure that I can help you answer them.

But here's the problem … I don't know what you don't know. That is often a real and very serious problem. One of the first things I do when I meet someone is ask a lot of questions. I have discovered over the years that a lot of people don't know what they don't know about financial matters. Others think that if they don't know something, it isn't a problem; if you don't know that you have cancer, it will still kill you. Just because you don't know something is a problem doesn't mean that it is *not* a problem. My goal is to help you identify the potential problems and give you the knowledge you need to come up with a solution.

There are some things that you can't know. Those things make financial planning very difficult. For instance, you can't know how long you're going to live. Everyone's birth certificate has an expiration date on it. The problem is that barring a planned suicide or a scheduled execution for a crime, we have no way of determining what your expiration date is. If somehow you could tell me what date you are going to die, I would be able to figure out how much money you would need to pay your bills, cover your living expenses, and even have enough to do some travel or play golf every week. I could tell you how much you needed to set aside and invest so that when you finally expired, you would go with your accounts current and one thin dime in your pocket. In the financial planning world, we jokingly call that good timing.

As I've said, people don't know what they don't know. And *I* don't know what they don't know either. All I know is that they feel like there's a pain, and it's in their retirement plan … or lack thereof. It's not a physical pain—at least not yet. It is a small nagging feeling of uneasiness about their future. And this concern is growing larger every day that passes. Oftentimes, this uneasiness comes from a lack of a plan or strategy about the future. Not knowing can in and of itself cause a lot of stress. They know they need to do something, but they aren't sure what that is. And in their perception, this vague lurking monster is instilling a level of fear in their minds.

When people are in this situation, it's usually because they feel like they don't have enough information, or they simply don't understand the information they do have. In some cases, they may not trust the information someone else has given them. Do they have to change their investments? Do they need to leave their current advisor? Should they change their strategies? There are lots of questions whirling around inside their heads, and the answers seem unattainable. And, unfortunately, not knowing can leave some of us paralyzed, which often leads to inaction, only enhancing the problem over time.

In my practice, my goal is to determine the facts and identify the cause of the pain. Is it even real? How bad is it? Once I do this, I can offer a solution; but first I must find out what it is that my clients know and do not know about how retirement works. Only then can I help them define their true financial goals. Once we establish that, we sometimes discover that they are in a good situation, and I send them on their way. I'm not going to take advantage of a client's lack of knowledge and make up a problem when one isn't there. The Lord has blessed me with plenty of clients. I don't need to make up problems they don't have or poach them from other advisors. My favorite thing in the world is to pat someone on the back and tell them how great of a job they've done.

The Reason

I have written this book to help educate you about the things that can wreck your retirement. This way, you can avoid the potholes I have often seen retirees fall into. I truly believe if more people understood what they need to know in order to have a successful retirement, we would all benefit. The present reality is that there are too many people who are not fully prepared for their retirement years, and they don't know what they need to be prepared. They just know something is wrong.

We all know someone who has gone to the doctor because they weren't feeling well. They think all they have is a cold or, at worst, that they're coming down with the flu. The doctor begins by asking them some questions and then does a preliminary examination. Because of their years of education and experience, the doctor realizes that there may indeed be something more serious behind their symptoms. If you were the patient, would you want your doctor to ignore his or her suspicions and just treat you for the flu because that's what *you* thought was wrong? Of course not. You would want the doctor to run some tests and zero in on what is really going on.

That's what I do when someone comes into my office with a vague feeling of financial distress. If my investigative process reveals that there is a bigger, more serious issue going on with your financial or retirement plan, then that's what we're going to talk about. You may have diversification issues with your portfolio. You may have an imbalance in your investment allocations. Your financial goals may have changed. You may be on your way to running out of money before you run out of life. Whatever it is, we are going to flesh it out so you can leave my office knowing that you have a plan. And you should expect no less from any advisor you choose to work with.

It is unfortunate that in today's world of poorly planned financial reality, we often see the too-little-too-late scenario where the person did not plan wisely and outlived his or her money. I had a new client come into my office years ago. Martha was a very healthy and alert woman of ninety-four, but she was sobbing as she sat across from me. Back at her eightieth birthday, she had sat down with her former financial guy. "I'm never going to make it to ninety years old," Martha had told him. "I'm still in good health, but I've outlived my parents by a long time. All my siblings are gone. I don't have any children. No one is left for whom I need to provide. I want to start drawing on my retirement and enjoying myself. Maybe do a little traveling. See the pyramids, visit Fiji. How much can I spend every year to make sure that I'm out of money by the time I'm ninety? I don't want to die with anything left but some great memories and a smile on my face."

Her financial advisor told her what I think most advisors would say. "Let's err on the side of caution, Martha. Let's plan your distributions out to age ninety-five."

She agreed that this sounded reasonable, so that's what they did.

Now, here she was at age ninety-four, sitting in my office in despair. Her financial plan had performed perfectly except for one thing: she didn't die. Martha had a well-stamped passport, a ton of photos, and great memories, but only one year's worth of money left in her account. She was still in great health, and the end was not even on the horizon.

It has been my experience that longevity is the number one killer of financial security. Some things you simply can't know. When you are going to die is one of them, and that makes planning somewhat difficult. You can't know when you're going to die or what your health is going to be when you finally reach the age when you want to slow down and take it easy, but you have to prepare for it. My philosophy is to always plan for the worst-case scenario. If you can live with the worst-case scenario, then you can live without worry. Ironically, the best-case scenario for you, health-wise—a long healthy life—is the worst-case scenario for you financially. We're rapidly approaching the point where people are living in retirement longer than they worked. And you must plan for this if you don't want to run out of money before you run out of life.

Thanks to advances in modern medicine, technology, and generally healthier lifestyles, centenarians are the fastest-growing age group by percentage.[1] Many people today who think they're not going to make it to one hundred are, in fact, going to make it there.

From my experience, most people tend to underestimate how long they're going to live. They also fail to take into account what effect their failing health is going to have on their retirement years. They are not prepared for many of the financial land mines that can blow up in their golden years.

I find that most people are good chess players; they're not great chess players, and they're certainly not master chess players. If you know anything about chess, a good chess player will think a couple of moves ahead. A great chess player generally thinks five, six moves ahead, but chess masters think seven or eight moves ahead. They anticipate what their opponent is going to do and how they are going to respond over the next seven or eight moves.

Most people are only good at planning their retirement, but they're not great, and they are certainly not masters. When they're sixty, they can think out to eighty-five years. When they're seventy, they can think out to eighty-five or ninety, but what about ninety to one hundred? If you've planned out to ninety but wind up living to one hundred, you may be in trouble. I have an aunt who died recently at 101 years old. I have a client whose mother recently passed away at the age of 106. My client was eighty.

We are seeing people live longer lives after retirement. You have to prepare for that. You have to plan as if you're going to live a long life. What will happen if you outlive your money? A lot of people will deflect the serious nature of that question because it is a very frightening prospect.

---

1   The Associated Press, "Centenarians Are the Fastest-Growing Age Segment: Number of 100-Year-Olds to Hit 6 Million by 2050," *Daily News*, July 21, 2009, https://www.nydailynews.com/life-style/centenarians-fastest-growing-age-segment-number-100-year-olds-hit-6-million-2050-article-1.400828.

"I'll just shoot myself," they will say jokingly.

The problem is they don't allow guns in nursing homes. It's just an unrealistic thing. We all want to die in our sleep, but there is no guarantee that it will be in our bed in our own home. Many people die in a bed in a nursing facility—not the ending they envisioned for their lives. Go visit the ten nearest nursing homes around your community. Ask any resident in there one question. "Do you want to be here?"

No one wants to be there. Many of these facilities are understaffed, underbudgeted, and doing all they can to meet the bare minimums of compassionate care. At best, it is like going to jail because you committed the crime of getting old. At worst, it is like being warehoused with all the other criminals.

I have a friend named Allen whose mother had a cerebral aneurysm but did not die. His father tried to take care of his wife the best he could in their small retirement home in Florida. He did so for several years as their savings slowly dwindled. Then Allen's father fell gravely ill and died. Allen had no choice but to put his own mother in a government-funded critical care facility.

He would go and visit her every Saturday, wheeling her down to the dayroom and talking to her, even though he knew she had no idea who he was or what he was saying. He noticed an elderly gentleman sitting alone at the same table every Saturday, holding a jigsaw puzzle piece in his hand as he stared down at the 999 other pieces on the table. One Saturday, Allen approached the man and discovered his name was George. He asked George if he could help him with the puzzle.

"I appreciate the offer, young man," said George. "But I think it's impossible. Somebody threw away the box that the puzzle came in. I don't know what the picture is supposed to look like."

Your life is like a puzzle, and every little piece has to fit in its place for you to have a clear picture of retirement. Most people have never thought about what their retirement picture is supposed to look like, much less how the individual pieces fit in. When people ask me when they should take their Social Security or if they should pay off their mortgage, I say I don't know. Those are individual pieces. I need to have a feel for what they want their retirement picture to look like. I need to know when they are planning to retire and whether they are planning to work after they retire from their current career. I need to know their health issues, their fears, and their concerns. Do they have a mortgage? Are they taking Social Security? What are their other sources of income? How much debt do they have? How much income do they have?

Will their income adjust for inflation?

I need to have all those puzzle pieces in front of me so I can then take the piece that they're asking about and put it in the right place. I can take your mortgage piece and put it in one section, and I can slide your Social Security piece into another section. Every piece has to fit where it belongs. Otherwise, the picture isn't clear. I ask a lot of questions to verify that I'm not missing anything, because if I'm missing even one piece of the puzzle, then the entire puzzle is off. It may not be devastating, but it also may not be the best way.

You can't know how long you're going to live, and you can't know how your health is going to be in your final years. So you must plan for a worst-case scenario.

The good news is that the rest of the book is dedicated to the things that you can know and what you should know, and how every piece fits into your retirement puzzle. By being better educated, you can prepare yourself for a worry-free retirement.

They say knowledge is power, but only applied knowledge is power. This book is not going to tell you what the secret herbs and spices are to have a successful financial plan. This book's not going to tell you that if you do this and this and don't do that, you'll never have to worry about running out of money. Why? Because I can't tell you that. Every person's situation is different. Every person is unique. Sometimes the difference between my recommendation to client A and client B is the result of how each one feels about a particular issue.

Proper financial planning is never a one-size-fits-all proposition. Two people may share the same tastes and philosophies, be in the same general socioeconomic classification, have the same education, and have traveled much the same road through life but can arrive at my doorstep with completely different circumstances.

You would be amazed at how many times someone will call to tell me about a crisis that has suddenly popped up because a family member or friend needs some financial help. For example, there was this couple who had done everything right. They had worked hard, built a business, made some smart moves along the way, and managed to do very well for themselves. They had put together a good, solid financial plan that was going to give them a comfortable retirement. They were just a few months from selling their business and heading off on a tour of Europe.

Everything was going according to what they had planned for this stage of their lives. Life, however, has this not-so-funny way of throwing you a fast one, high and tight, when you're

Proper financial planning is never a one-size-fits-all proposition.

expecting a slider hanging out over the plate. If you're not a baseball fan and don't understand the metaphor ... it means you are about to get hit in the head by the pitch.

The wife's sister called her in desperation, begging for help. The brother-in-law had lost his job, there was very little money in their savings account, and they couldn't make the house or car payment and still have enough money for groceries. They just needed a loan to get them by until the brother-in-law could find another job. While it was tragic and desperate for the sister, the request would require the couple to dip into their retirement nest egg.

When my clients call me with a troubling situation like this, they do not need someone to jump on the emotional bandwagon with them. They need an objective advisor who is going to act upon his or her fiduciary obligation and give them objective advice.

Fiduciary refers to the legal obligation of someone entrusted with the care of someone's money or property to act in the best interest of that party. And as both an investment advisor and attorney, I have a fiduciary duty to act in my client's best interest. Additionally, you should also know that I am a born-again Christian who has given my life to my Lord and Savior, Jesus Christ, and I adhere to biblical principles in both my personal and professional life. I believe in charity and tithing and giving to the poor. I also believe in living a responsible and upstanding life.

This couple had a serious dilemma. They wanted to help the wife's sister, but it meant taking from their retirement. Had they been my clients, I would have started, as I always do, by asking them questions. Why did the brother-in-law lose his job? He had a good job and was making good money, so why don't they have any savings? Just as I don't know what you don't know when you come to me as a new client, I remind my clients to adopt the same practice to gather the facts so they can properly assess the situation. Be vigilant.

This was what this couple did. They investigated and asked questions. When all the facts came to light, it turned out that the brother-in-law had lost his job because he was at the horse track instead of at work. He had a very serious gambling addiction and had burned through the family's savings. Now his family was suffering because he refused to recognize that he had a problem. He was looking for someone to bail him out so he wouldn't have to accept responsibility.

I heard a saying once about personal responsibility that fits this example. "You are where you are, at any given point in your life, because of a series of choices that you have made. If you don't like where you are, make better choices."

There are bigger issues at work here than a temporary financial setback. Choosing to ignore the warning signs of destructive behavior has consequences. Choosing to make irresponsible financial choices in your life is your responsibility, not someone else's.

If they had been my clients, I would have advised them to buy the family some groceries. I might even have suggested they take in the sister and her children for a while so the brother-in-law could get the help he needed; but in no way would I have advised them to dip into their retirement savings to bail the brother-in-law out of his mess. You must rescue shipwreck survivors, but you cannot allow a sinking ship to suck you down too. Some of you are probably thinking that sounds very cold and greedy; however, it's reasonable and responsible. I was raised to be responsible and to make good choices in life, and that is how I raise my own children. It has been my observation that most successful people can say the same. Our world is reeling today from too many people growing up thinking they do not need to take personal responsibility for their actions. There comes a time when you are an adult and you have made a mess that you have to clean up. You do not show that you love someone by allowing them to avoid the consequences of their actions. That is not love; that is enabling. At some point, people must take responsibility for their lives.

Your child may want you to pay for college so he doesn't have to apply for student loans. That is a very common temptation that many parents face today. Unless you are wealthy enough to give them the money and not have it affect your retirement, I would advise against this. Your child can finance college, and he will have his entire life to pay off student loans; you, on the other hand, cannot finance retirement. Nothing exists financially in a vacuum. Actions have consequences. Just as what you don't know can hurt you, what you choose to do or not do can also cause you pain.

Fortunately, there are things you can know, and that is what this book is going to talk about. With a little bit of education, you'll be able to plan for your future financial success. This is not going to be a financial planning book that says if you do *A*, *B* and *C*, everything is going to be fine. It can't be done that way, because there are things you can't know that will cause you to have to prepare for the worst.

It is my sincere hope that in reading this book, you will take the time to stop and think about what the picture of your life is supposed to look like when you get into the sunset years. What you don't know can cause you to end up someplace that you would never want to be. I have written this book to help guide you as you piece together the puzzle of your financial life. My prayer is that when you sit down with your financial planner, you will be able to describe in detail what your picture is supposed to look like so they can help you put those pieces in the right places for a successful retirement.

CHAPTER TWO

What You Don't Know about Financial Planning

LET'S IMAGINE FOR a moment that you have found the perfect piece of property upon which you want to build your dream home. The location is perfect, the view is breathtaking, and you were able to purchase it at fair market value. You walk into the local residential contractor's office with a copy of the mortgage survey, and you slap it on his desk.

"I just bought this lot," you announce proudly. "I want you to build me a house."

"That's a fairly large lot," he says, studying the lot dimensions. "What kind of house are you looking for?"

"Oh, you know, just a house. Some bedrooms, a nice kitchen, a couple bathrooms, and a two-car garage."

"What is your budget? That lot is located in a deed-restricted development."

"What does that mean?"

"Well, in this particular development, it means your home has to be designed by a licensed architect, and your plans have to be submitted to the homeowner's association for approval. The exterior has to be stone and wood."

"Wait a minute. I have to hire an architect?"

The absurdity of this situation and the lack of forethought and planning on the part of the property owner are what financial advisors face nearly every day. There are important events in our lives that require us to think, research, consult professionals, and make tough choices. Building a custom dream home is one. Planning your retirement years should be another. You would not think about building a home without, at a minimum, having a floor plan and an exterior view that you had pulled from a magazine or plan book. But I have spoken with people in my office who have given more thought to the name of their new puppy than they have to how they are going to finance their lifestyle after they retire from their jobs.

Unfortunately, most people have never taken time to figure out what the goal is for their money. What is its purpose? What do you want it to do for you? If you don't know the purpose for your money, how do you know if your current strategy is supporting or conflicting that purpose? If you have never set a target, how do you know if you've hit it? Or if you've missed it? Because most people have never given this much thought, this is one of the first discussions I have with a new client. We need to crystallize their goals so we can develop a strategy and a financial plan to support them.

Unless you are a contractor, you would rarely consider building a house on your own and never without a blueprint or goal in mind. Yet I repeatedly talk with folks who try to do their own financial planning. They make the decisions about when to take their Social Security without investigating the options available to them. They make decisions about how much they can withdraw from their portfolio based upon a magazine article they read in the doctor's waiting room. They make decisions about their investments based upon tips from their hairdresser who got her information from another customer who has a cousin whose son just graduated from college and got a job with a nationally known discount broker. My sister, Denise Johnson, is a hairdresser; Denise is not going to pretend to be able to give her customers financial advice just because I am her brother. She's probably going to give them my business card.

Do-it-yourself financial planning can be very expensive in the long run. As we will uncover in the chapter on Social Security, if you don't know what you are doing, you can leave hundreds of thousands of dollars in Uncle Sam's account that should rightfully be in your account. You can get locked into an investment that costs you more than you earned to liquidate. Or you can lose a lot of money. Unless you are a financial advisor who deals with these issues every day, there are many things you don't know about establishing a financial plan.

When we talk about a financial plan, we are referring to your investment plan and your income plan. The plan as a whole should include investment strategies and tactics that will help you reach your goal.

The investment plan should cover the best way to invest your portfolio so that it supports your financial plan. It must reflect the realities of the economic environment in which you live. It has to reflect whether you are in the accumulation phase of your life or in the distribution stage. If you're in the accumulation phase and your goal is growth, then the investment plan should be designed particularly around investments that are more geared toward growth, like stocks and mutual funds. If you're in the retirement phase and the goal of your plan is to withdraw funds from your accounts so you can pay the bills each month, then your investments need to include a

When we talk about a financial plan, we are referring to your invest-ment plan and your income plan. The plan as a whole should include investment strategies and tactics that will help you reach your goal.

variety that produces income so you can withdraw the cash you need while leaving your principal intact. An investment plan answers the question, "How should I invest my funds to best support my goal?"

Income planning has to do with the best way to get your income once you reach the dis-tribution phase of life. It helps maximize your income while minimizing your taxes so that you can have the peace of mind of never having to worry about outliving your money. An income plan answers the question, "How am I going to take the income from my portfolio?"

If you have securities, stocks, or bonds that you have to liquidate in order to get your income, that's an important piece of the puzzle. If you have a large enough stash to be able to live off the interest and dividends without touching your principal, we must consider that as well. If you have annuities in your plan with income riders, then we have to strategize a schedule to turn those income riders on. Do we draw down one account while letting other accounts grow? We have to know when Social Security is going to come into play. Do you file at sixty-two or at your full retirement age? Or do you wait until you're seventy? If you have retirement accounts, where does the income come from? Does it all come from your retirement accounts? Does it all come from your taxable accounts or a combination of each? If one spouse passes away, will the other spouse still have enough income to survive?

That's all part of your income planning.

The financial plan takes all of these pieces of the puzzle and puts them together in the right places so you have a clear picture of how you're going to make it through the rest of your life without running out of money. The plan basically says, "Here are all my assets. Here is the amount I want to take from my portfolio. This is how I am going to take it. This is when and how I am going to take Social Security. This is how my required minimum distributions are going to come into play. This is how I am going to invest my retirement until I need it." That's the financial plan in general, but the assets must be invested so they support your goals. That requires a seasoned professional who can survey the financial landscape and help you chart a course from where you are now to where you want to be. There are many minefields and hidden obstacles along the way. Your financial advisor is trained to help you recognize and avoid pitfalls like taxes, fees, and interest rate fluctuations. Let's examine some of these so you understand the challenges ahead.

Let's Talk About Taxes

Not having a basic understanding of the tax code could cause you to pay needless taxes or pay more taxes than necessary. There are seven different federal income tax rates for tax year 2021.

2022 FEDERAL INCOME TAX RATES		
Percentage Rate	Income Level – Single	Income Level – Married Filing Jointly
10 percent	$0 to $10,275	$0 to $20,550
12 percent	$10,276 to $41,775	$20,551 to $83,550
22 percent	$41,776 to $89,075	$83,551 to $178,150
24 percent	$89,076 to $170,050	$178,151 to $340,100
32 percent	$170,051 to $215,950	$340,101 to $431,900
35 percent	$215,951 to $539,900	$431,901 to $647,850
37 percent	$539,901 or more	$647,851 or more

Source: https://www.irs.gov/newsroom/
irs-provides-tax-inflation-adjustments-for-tax-year-2022

TABLE A

Most people don't understand that we're in a progressive tax society. This means that if you're in the top tax bracket, which is 37 percent today, then you're still going to pay 10 percent on the first $19,900 of taxable income if you're a joint filer. Many people think that if you're in the 37 percent tax bracket, you pay 37 percent on all of your income. That is simply not true. Allow me to illustrate how it really works.

Let's suppose bachelor millionaire Harry Hedgefund, who is in the 37 percent tax bracket, uses all his allowed exemptions and deductions and ends up with an annual taxable income of $1 million. If he were paying a proportional type of tax rate, he would write a check to the IRS for 37 percent of $1 million, or $370,000. When we think of it in a progressive tax structure, he would pay the following:

2022 FEDERAL INCOME TAX—H. HEDGEFUND FILING SINGLE ON $1,000,000 INCOME		
Percentage Rate	Income Level - Single	Tax Owed
10 percent	Less Than $10,275	$1,027.50
12 percent	$10,276 to $41,775	$3,779.88
22 percent	$41,776 to $89,075	$10,405.70
24 percent	$89,076 to $170,050	$19,433.76
32 percent	$170,051 to $215,950	$14,687.68
35 percent	$215,951 to $539,900	$113,382.15
37 percent	$539,901 or more	$170,263.63
Estimated Total Tax Owed		$332,953.30

TABLE B

The difference is $35,011, or 9.6 percent less than just making it a simple, straightforward calculation. Rule of thumb: there is nothing simple or straightforward about the federal tax code. There's a reason they call it the tax code; it has to be cracked. Trying to crack it on your own can be very expensive.

Because people don't really understand taxes, they're not as aggressive with their tax planning as they should be. A Roth IRA conversion is a good example. The biggest gap in our current tax code is the gap between 12 percent and 22 percent. It is a 10 percent difference. You can, as a married couple over sixty-five years old, make up to $81,051 a year of taxable income and never leave the 12 percent tax bracket. A lot of people don't realize that. Because of this, they don't do things like Roth conversions. That is something that could help them dramatically. They don't take advantage of the tax code. If you can convert $20,000–$30,000 a year from an IRA to a Roth IRA and never leave the 12 percent tax bracket, that's a good deal.

Another very important thing that many people don't understand is Social Security tax. You are sadly mistaken if you think that you are done with the IRS and federal income taxes when you retire and draw Social Security benefits. You need to have a basic understanding of how Social Security taxes work.

If you don't make a certain amount of "provisional" income, you don't have to pay taxes on Social Security. To calculate your provisional income, you must first compute your adjusted gross income without Social Security benefits. You then add together your computed adjusted gross income (AGI), tax-free interest (aka municipal bond interest), and one-half of your Social Security benefits. Provisional income falling below the base amount established by your filing status is untaxed. Taxes are due only if your provisional income is above the base amount.

Sometimes I find that a client is making too much provisional income solely because they have their investments appropriated incorrectly. It causes their income to show up on the tax return, whereas if they just repositioned a few things, it wouldn't show up on their tax return at all, and they could lower their overall income. Consequently, they could reduce or eliminate the tax they are paying on their Social Security just by repositioning the pieces of their puzzle.

If you are married and make under $32,000 a year of provisional income, you pay no taxes on Social Security. If you make somewhere between $32,000 and $44,000 a year, you pay taxes on up to half of your Social Security. If you make over $44,000 a year, then the amount of your Social Security that is taxed jumps up to 85 percent. So, if 85 percent of your Social Security is $40,000, you've got to claim that $40,000 as income. If your marginal tax bracket is 22 percent, you are going to pay $8,800 of tax on Social Security that should never have been taxed in the first place. If you are a single filer and are at the top of the 12 percent tax bracket notwithstanding your Social Security income, you will pay roughly $4,500 in taxes. If you file for Social Security and begin collecting $40,000 per year, your tax bill will almost triple to nearly $12,000 per year! What you didn't know about Social Security taxes cost you $7,500. This makes April 15 less pleasant than it already is. A good financial plan would have spotted that land mine beforehand, and you could have defused it.

Another trip wire in this area is the required minimum distribution (RMD) provisions. The RMD is taxed as ordinary income. I've often seen retirees take their RMD without realizing that it may push them into another tax bracket. Plus, having this additional income may create a domino effect by causing them to have to pay more taxes on their Social Security income. This will be another unpleasant surprise come Tax Day.

An illustration may best help you understand the impact of the Social Security tax and why it is so sneaky.

Let's suppose you take a dollar out of your retirement account to live off or to satisfy your required minimum distribution. Let's also assume that you're in the 22 percent tax bracket. You take a dollar; you've got to pay 22 cents on that dollar, right? But because you took that dollar, you might now have to include another 85 cents of income from Social Security. So, add 85 cents from Social Security to the front of your tax return. You've only taken a dollar, but you've got to pay taxes on the $1.85. So, 22 percent on the first dollar is 22 cents, but 22 percent on the additional $0.85 of Social Security income is 19 cents. So, you take 22 cents, and you add 19 cents to it, ultimately costing you 41 cents in tax, all because you took one dollar. You took one dollar; you've got to pay 41 cents of tax. That's 41 percent, folks! That's higher than the highest tax bracket in the United States tax code. Jeff Bezos, founder of Amazon, isn't taking Social Security. Jeff

Bezos pays only 37 percent, but you, as a retiree, are special. You get to pay 41 percent of tax on your distributions.

That's what I mean when I refer to this as a sneaky tax. And we haven't even talked about state income tax. California has the highest state income tax at 12.3 percent on more than $1,250,738 for married joint filers and $1 million for those filing individually.[2]

When you add the state tax to the 41 percent federal tax that you've just paid, you may very well wind up paying over 50 percent in total taxes! All because you took a dollar from your retirement accounts.

The next time someone says, "You know, I don't want to make more money, because I might have to pay half of it in tax," they may not be lying.

Interest Rates

People often ask me where I think interest rates are going to go. They also want to know how interest rates are going to affect their portfolio. There seems to be a general lack of understanding of basic economic principles in the world today. I don't believe that a lot of people understand how interest rates affect the general economy overall. The majority of people believe that the Federal Reserve System is part of the federal government. They don't know that it is really a private entity: the bank's bank.

The Federal Reserve System was given three mandates when it was established in 1913. These were maximizing employment, stabilizing prices, and moderating long-term interest rates. Over the years, the three mandates have been reduced simply to maximizing employment and controlling inflation.

---

2   Bankrate.com, "California State Taxes 2021-2022: Income and Sales Tax Rates," December 23, 2021, https://www.bankrate.com/taxes/california-state-taxes/.

Instead, the Fed has become the effective loan shark to the spend-thrift US Congress. The Fed uses "monetary policy" to determine the amount of money and credit in the US economy. The Fed lends this money, or "legal tender," to the banks for a portion of the interest rate the bank is charging the consumer.

To create the legal tender, the Fed buys and sells securities, which are almost always backed by the "full faith and credit" of the US government. This buying and selling is known as "open market operations" and is the primary tool of the Fed's monetary policy. The rate of interest that the Federal Reserve sets for the banks for their short-term loans is called "the Fed Funds rate."

The Fed Funds rate tells an untold story. People are surprised when I tell them that I don't believe the economy is doing as well as everyone says. One reason for this is based on interest rates and how it is that low interest rates have been the driver of this decade-long bull market. But I believe that the story it tells is much different than the story you've heard. And I don't believe it will have a happy ending. If you're up for a long story, a perspective that you probably haven't ever considered, then buckle up.

In 2000, the Fed Funds rate, the overnight rate from bank to bank, was at 6 percent. When the dot-com crash happened, the Fed dropped that rate down to zero. People who were heavily invested in tech stocks watched much of their net worth get washed away. Banks had to engage in a type of shell game, moving cash around to make sure local banks could meet their reserve requirements. From 2002 to 2007, the market came back, and the Fed raised rates back up to almost 6 percent.

When the market crashed again in 2008, once again the Fed dropped the rate down to zero, but this time, it didn't work; it didn't stop the crash. Because the market kept crashing, the government had to pull out another weapon in their arsenal. They started printing money. They didn't call it *printing money*, because that would be pretty obvious. Plus, most people call that counterfeiting. The Federal Reserve called it *quantitative easing*. But why did the Fed print money? What was the goal? Most average Joes can't answer this question.

The basic premise is that, by printing money, the Fed, through the banking system, floods the markets with an excess supply of cash. With excess cash on hand, banks will lower interest rates to entice corporations and consumers to borrow those funds so they can put the cash to use. If corporations and consumers borrow this cash, then they will spend it. If they spend these funds, then it will increase corporate revenues. As corporate revenues increase, corporate profits will increase. If corporate profits increase, then the stock prices should start to rise. If stock prices rise, then the crash will end. Sounds good, right? What's the big deal? How about that, as a result of this practice, our country accrued more debt over the last decade than it has over its entire history? That's the big deal! Someone's got to pay it back, right?

But did it work? Did the Fed's quantitative easing programs over the next six years stall the crash and restore the economy? I believe that is arguable. The question open for debate is whether the Fed's printing of money staved off further market declines or whether the crash of 2008 had run its course and would have ended anyway. No one can say for sure.

But here are two things that we do know for sure. First, our country was in $10.63 trillion of debt on Obama's inauguration day in 2009,[3] and now we owe more than $29 trillion.[4] Our national

---

3   The Balance, "National Debt under Obama," https://www.thebalance.com/national-debt-under-obama-3306293.

4   Truth in Accounting, "Our Debt Clock," December 23, 2021, https://www.truthinaccounting.org/about/our_national_debt?gclid=CjwKCAjw3riIBhAwEiwAzD3TiQkb61G36F66MVRHvrqP-ySiIQE6hzCGQN-EUxUhKG0X2Dl3_V924RoCTuwQAvD_BwE.

debt has nearly tripled in the last thirteen years! Granted, roughly $8 trillion of this debt is because of the COVID stimulus packages that I discuss later. Even prior to COVID, though, our national debt more than doubled over a decade. Secondly, and even more telling, is that the Fed Funds rate, which the Fed lowered from around 6 percent in 2007 to zero by 2009, is still near zero. In 2000, before the dot-com bust of 2001, the Fed Funds rate was at 6 percent. But the Fed lowered it to zero by 2002 to stave off that crash. By 2007, the Fed had raised it back to almost 6 percent, as they should have, because the economy had fully recovered. However, between 2007 and 2009, because the subprime mortgage debacle caused the market to crash by more than 60 percent, the Fed once again lowered the rates back to zero. Now that the stock market has fully recovered and then some, where are rates currently at? We're thirteen years and one pandemic into this recovery, and everyone is shouting how great the economy is doing while pointing to the record highs of the stock market. Therefore, the Fed has raised rates back to 6 percent, right? Wrong.

The Fed Funds rate is still near zero! And the $64,000 question is, why? Why has the Federal Reserve System not raised the rate back to 6 percent, where it was in 2000 and 2007? Good question. The Fed has been telling us they have suppressed rates because inflation remained stubbornly low, under 2 percent. At the same time, they're saying the economy is as strong as ever and consumers are spending more money than ever despite COVID. But these statements contradict each other. You can't have a strong economy and a low inflation rate at the same time. Economics doesn't work that way. A low inflation rate is even worse for an economy than a high inflation rate, and the Fed wants inflation to rise before raising rates. That's their side of the story. But the lack of inflation tells another side. Inflation occurs when there is a greater supply of money than goods. If this supply of money is chasing these goods, the cost of the goods will increase. It's a simple Economics 101, supply-and-demand equation. If there is a demand for the goods, prices will rise. If there is not a huge demand for the goods, prices will not rise.

EFFECTIVE FEDERAL FUNDS RATE JULY 1954 TO JULY 2022

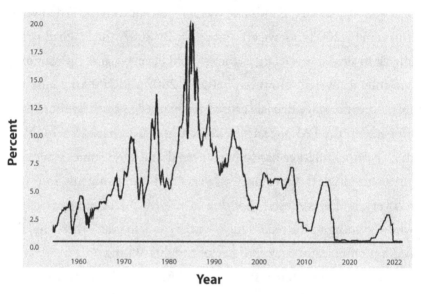

Source: Board of Governors of the Federal Reserve System (US)   fred.stlouisfed.org

CHART A

But this creates a dilemma for the Fed; an economy does well when consumers spend money. If consumers spend money, it increases the demand for products, which causes prices to rise. If prices rise, then there is inflation. Therefore, if there is no inflation, it boils down to the fact that consumers are not spending money. Hence, a reduced demand for the goods and services being offered by businesses today. But this is not what we're being told. The media reports that the consumer is strong and spending money like never before. If this were true, then prices would rise. But prices aren't rising, and inflation is low, or so we're being told.

I believe there's more to this story—the rest of the story, as Paul Harvey used to say. The government wants to position the economy as being great, the best it's ever been. They don't want inflation, but they can't have it both ways: a good economy and no inflation. If the economy is good, there will be inflation.

This leads to another question, though: Is it true that the economy is not expanding as we're being told, hence the lack of inflation? Or could it be true that the economy is really humming along, but the government is only telling us there is no inflation when in fact there is? These are the only two options, right? Either the economy is not doing so good, which is why there is no inflation, or the economy is actually doing well but the government is only telling us there is no inflation. But does the government *really* want there to be inflation? If inflation is a sign of a healthy economy, because there is a high demand for goods and services, why would the government *not want* inflation?

Here's one reason: The government pays your Social Security checks. Isn't there a cost-of-living adjustment tied to your Social Security checks each year that is correlated to inflation? As inflation grows, so does your Social Security check. Do you see where this is going?

There are 65 million Americans collecting Social Security,[5] which amounts to about one out of every five people. Plus, there are ten thousand baby boomers retiring and filing for Social Security benefits every day. That's over 3.6 million new recipients each year and a grand total of over 54 million new Social Security recipients over the next decade and a half. If the government has to provide a cost-of-living adjustment on every one of these Social Security benefits every year to adjust for inflation, do they want inflation to be high? Of course not!

---

5   Fact Sheet, "Social Security," December 23, 2021, https://www.ssa.gov/news/press/factsheets/basicfact-alt.pdf.

I don't believe that the real reason the Fed hasn't raised rates is because of low inflation. I do believe the real reason is because our government does not want to increase your Social Security benefits as is required if inflation grows. So, they tell us there is no inflation. But ask yourself this: Do you find that the goods and services you buy cost the same as they did five years ago? Ten years ago? I don't believe the Fed's story of low inflation can last forever, though. At some point soon, we'll likely see inflation numbers start to rise—possibly in a big way.

But there's more: a low inflation rate benefits the government in another major way. The government is now $29 trillion in debt. Let me ask you, If you happened to owe $29 trillion on a credit card, would you want rates to be high or low? Silly question, right? Every time the Fed raises rates a quarter point, do you realize that it will cost the government about $72.5 billion per year in additional interest? If interest rates go back to the level they were at in 2000 and 2007, it would cost the government an additional $1.7 trillion in interest each and every year! So you be the judge: Does the government want inflation, and hence interest rates, to be high or low?

Here's the clincher. The Fed has always been able to keep the economy stable by raising and lowering interest rates. If the economy gets overheated, the Fed raises rates, making it more expensive for corporations and consumers to borrow money, causing them to spend less. If the economy needs a boost, the Fed lowers rates to encourage consumers and corporations to borrow money and increase spending.

What has been the result of all the Fed's financial shenanigans on the stock market? As of mid-2021, it is sitting at record highs. The last dozen years have produced annualized double digit returns for stocks. The question is, How long will it last? Even if you don't know a thing about economics, from purely a common sense point of view, does anything go up forever? You know the answer. If the stock market has another major correction, how is the Fed going to deal with it? They can't lower interest rates because they are already near historic lows. They've already printed over $8 trillion of stimulus to keep our country out of a depression because of COVID, so this is the last thing they'd want to do. In other words, the Fed is out of bullets, and this is a major reason to be concerned.

The printing of money and inserting it into an economy is artificial. If your lifestyle is great, but only because I'm giving you money every month, that's artificially great. You're not producing anything. You're not contributing anything. You're not making something. You're not selling anything. There's no economic benefit for you. You're just taking the money and spending it. How long can this go on for? And what happens when I stop giving you money? When you print money and give it to an economy, that's what's happening. The Fed has given the economy trillions of dollars to prop up the economic system. Don't misunderstand me: I believe all the recent stimulus has been absolutely necessary to keep our country from going into a major depression because of COVID. I also believe it has to end at some point. The foundation of the recovery of 2009 started on an artificial foundation, and the stock market's growth over the last year and a half has also been built on a false foundation.

The printing of money, though, is not the only artificial maneuver that has helped our stock market continue to climb to record levels over the last dozen years. There have been some other artificial maneuvers that have also assisted in this recovery. If not for this artificial sleight of hand, I believe our economy would have had a major correction several years ago. It's good for an economy to have booms and busts. It's normal.

Let's talk about another recent manipulation that the Fed has encouraged. During the few years prior to the COVID meltdown and recovery, what do you think was the primary driver of the stock market growth? Was it consumer spending? Nope. What about increasing corporate profits? Wrong again. The primary driver of the new market highs was stock buybacks. Most people have heard the term but can't articulate what it really means, the impact it has on the economy, or even why companies buy back their own stock in the first place. Let's take a few minutes to flesh this out.

When a company buys back its own stock, there are two results. First, it creates an artificial demand for the stock; second, it creates an artificial increase in the company's earnings per share.

Let's talk about the stock price. The reason that a stock price increases is because there are more shares being bought than sold. In other words, the demand for the stock is greater than the supply.

When the demand increases, so does the price, just like inflation. When a company buys back its own stock, it creates a demand for that stock, which causes the price to rise. But are these upticks in the stock price a result of fundamental influences in the market, or would you say it is artificial? The fundamental way for a stock price to grow occurs when the company is growing. As it grows, the revenues increase, and the value of the company expands. The stock price will increase as a result. But when a company buys back its own stock, they have not added any new clients or sold any additional goods or services, yet they have caused the stock price to rise. It's artificial. And yet this has been one of the primary drivers of why stocks reached record levels prior to COVID.

But there's more. When a company buys back its own shares, it also causes the earnings per share (EPS) to grow. The EPS is an important measure that helps investors determine the health of a company. The higher the earnings are for a company, the higher the EPS. The higher the earnings are for each share of stock, the healthier the company. Or at least this is the way it is supposed to be.

There are only two ways for the EPS to increase: the fundamental way and the artificial way. If a company sells more stuff or takes on new subscribers, they increase the earnings. Hence the earnings per share increase. If the number of shares of outstanding stock remains constant but the company's earnings have increased, then their earnings per share will increase. This is the fundamental way for the EPS to grow.

Here's an example. Let's say that company A has earnings of $10 for every share of outstanding stock. Their earnings per share would be 10 ($10 divided by one share of stock). But let's assume that the company has doubled its revenues so that now it has earnings of $20 for every share of outstanding stock. The EPS would have risen to 20 ($20 divided by one share of stock), because the company doubled its revenues. This is good.

The other way to increase the EPS is to decrease the number of shares of stock. When a company buys back its own stock, it reduces the number of shares. If a company's earnings stay the same but the number of outstanding shares of stock is reduced, the EPS will go up. The company has not sold another product or taken on a new subscriber. Actually, the company has not taken in one dollar of additional revenue, yet the EPS has gone up, making it appear that the company has done better than it really has.

Let's consider another example. Company B has earnings of $20 for every two shares of outstanding stock the company has. Therefore, the earnings per share is 10 ($20 divided by two shares of stock). But now the company buys back half of its shares of stock. The result is that Company B now has earnings of $20 for each share of stock, which causes the EPS to increase to 20 ($20 of earnings divided by one share of stock). By buying back its own stock, the company has increased its EPS. But would you say that this increase in the earnings per share is a fundamental increase, or would you say it is artificial? Definitely artificial. Yet this was a primary driver of stock prices over the few years prior to COVID.

But there's more. You may be wondering where companies are getting the money to buy back their own shares. Short answer is that they're borrowing it. Why? Because the Fed has kept interest rates artificially low for the last decade. More than 80 percent of the companies that make up the S&P 500 have a stock buyback program in place. Over half of the $800 billion of share buybacks have been funded with borrowed money. As a result, corporate debt has swelled to a new record of roughly $10 trillion. This accounts for about 48 percent of the overall economy.

Why would corporations go into such dangerous levels of debt by borrowing money to buy back their own shares? Don't they know debt is bad? Good questions. Unfortunately, the answer is not so good. Over half of the companies in the S&P 500 compensate their executives based on the EPS of the company. Yes, that's right. The higher the EPS of these companies, the more the executives make. Certainly a conflict of interest. These companies are supposed to be acting in the best interest of the shareholders: Is borrowing their way to record levels of debt good or bad for shareholders? You know the answer.

Let's look at a real-life example. McDonald's is a good example to use for our conversation, because they have done a lot of buybacks.[6] From 2014 to 2016, McDonald's bought back $20.5 billion of their own stock. Yet during the same time, their net revenue was nearly $14 billion. That's a whopping 146 percent of its net revenue used to buy back its own shares.

---

6 *Forbes*, "McDonald's: Burgers, Fries and Stock Buybacks," April 27, 2017, https://www.forbes.com/sites/aalsin/2017/04/27/mcdonalds-burgers-fries-and-stock-buybacks/?sh=63da97c46266.

During the same period, McDonald's debt had increased from $14.1 billion to $25.9 billion—an increase of over 78 percent. Yet their revenue over that same time continuously declined from $28.1 billion to $24.6 billion—a decrease of over 12 percent.

Let me ask you, If a company's debt increased by 78 percent, and their revenues over the same time period decreased by 12 percent, what should the stock price do—go up or go down? You don't need to have financial acumen or know anything about economics or stocks to know that if a company's debt increases and revenue decreases, it should have a negative effect on the price of the stock. But is that what happened? You probably know the answer. The stock price did not go down. In the middle of 2013, McDonald's stock traded around $100 per share.[7] But three years later, the stock price had increased by a whopping 25 percent. Because McDonald's bought back so many of its own shares, the stock price increased despite the horrible fundamentals of the corporation.

I should also mention that 80 percent of a McDonald's executive's pay is based on the EPS, which they directly caused to go up as a result of the share buybacks. The Wall Street greed is back. It's the same thing that we saw with mortgages back in 2008. Credit default swaps, derivatives, and all the other financial sleights of hand that led to the 2007–2008 crisis are going on again. Unless some fundamental changes are made, we cannot expect a different result.

Yes, stock buybacks have been a primary driver of the growth in the stock market over the last few years.[8] Now that you know a little

---

7   Google Finance, "McDonald's Corp," https://www.google.com/finance/quote/ MCD:NYSE?window=MAX.

8   MarketWatch, "Buybacks Are the 'Dominant' Source of Stock Market Demand, and They Are Fading Fast: Goldman Sachs," https://www.marketwatch.com/story/ buybacks-are-the-dominant-source-of-stock-market-demand-and-they-are-fading-fast-goldman-sachs-2019-11-06.

more about them, would you say that they are a fundamental way for the stock market to grow? Or would you say it is more artificial? The problem with this bull market that has produced an annualized double-digit return over the last dozen years is that it has been built on an artificial foundation. It started in 2008, when the Fed started printing money. Because the Fed has kept interest rates low, it has encouraged the kind of stock buyback activity that has continued to artificially prop up the market. But can corporations keep buying back their own stock forever? Of course not, and when the buybacks end, the party will be over. What will happen then? It's anyone's guess. But it certainly has potential to end ugly.

If you don't know this information, you may very well end up as a casualty, like so many others who failed to make it through the crashes of 2001 and 2008. The good news is that it doesn't have to end ugly for you. Unfortunately, most people are asking the wrong question—a question that really doesn't matter for the immediate future. Where is the market going to go from here? That's what everyone wants to know. It doesn't matter one iota whether the market will go up or down in the future. That may come as a surprise because, after all, shouldn't everyone care what direction the stock market is headed in? No! The only reason you would care about where the market is going is if a move in the wrong direction is going to hurt you. If you are invested properly for the stage of life you are in, it does not matter.

Does anyone know for sure in what direction stocks are going from where they are today? Of course not. Now, over the long run, we can conclude that they are likely to go up, but over the short run, nobody knows. If you have a properly drafted financial plan, then it shouldn't matter where the market goes from here.

If you are in the accumulation phase of life, and you have at least fifteen years to go before you may need to start withdrawing funds from your portfolio, do you care what the market is going to do in the short run? It doesn't matter, so why ask the question?

But what you do know with absolute certainty is that the market is going to fluctuate. There are going to be smooth times and volatile times, good times and bad times. But if you're investing for the long run, why would you care about what you can't know? If you're basing your financial plan on what the market is going to do in the near future, you have the wrong financial plan and you're gambling.

What if you have less than a decade to retirement? Or if you're already in the distribution phase of life and taking withdrawals from your portfolio? What is the right question to ask yourself? Where is the market going? No. The right question is, Can you afford to take the risk? Can you withstand a 50 percent loss in your portfolio? Because every day you are in the market, your portfolio is exposed to that risk. When COVID hit our economy, the market dropped 37 percent in a little over five weeks![9] This was the fastest decline in US stock market history. It was also the third major crash the market has witnessed in the last two decades. This time, the market recovered in short order, but will we be so fortunate next time?

Prior to the COVID crash, we've had two other crashes close to 50 percent or more in the last twenty years. What will happen to your retirement plans if the market has another scenario similar to what happened in 2008, and it takes years to recover? Can you afford to take that chance? If you're in the accumulation phase of life, you can ride it out. As a matter of fact, a volatile market helps you if you're consistently buying stocks or mutual funds through your retirement accounts. But if you're in the distribution phase of life or close to it,

---

9   *Forbes*, "The Coronavirus Crash of 2020 and the Investing Lesson It Taught Us," February 11, 2021, https://www.forbes.com/sites/lizfrazierpeck/2021/02/11/the-coro-navirus-crash-of-2020-and-the-investing-lesson-it-taught-us/?sh=40b1afb146cf.

can you afford to gamble your retirement on where the market is likely to go in the short run? Most people can't. Warren Buffett has said, "If you aren't willing to own a stock for ten years, don't even think about owning it for ten minutes."

Retirees need to be asking themselves if they can afford to take a risk instead of pondering where the market will go. If you feel like you can't afford to take a risk, then I'm going to give you a sage piece of advice. Don't take the risk! Why gamble if you can't afford to lose? Having a well-thought-out financial plan will help you develop a strategy that will work for you no matter what the market does in the short run. You can do this with an educated advisor who has an idea of what the future risks may be. Many investors, retirees, and even financial advisors have never taken the time to learn what you just learned. They've simply never dug this deep. And if you or your advisor creates a financial plan based on a false set of assumptions, then you might as well deposit it into the round file immediately after it has been drafted. Your thoughts and philosophies must be taken into consideration when developing your financial plan. And if you or your advisor are assuming that the next dozen years are going to be as good as the last dozen, you may be building your financial plan on a foundation of sand. We all know people who planned on retiring in 2008 but couldn't because the subprime mortgage wave washed away their foundation.

Because we work almost exclusively with retirees or those who are within a decade of retirement, my firm specializes in fixed income, which is a necessity at this stage of life. Retirees need to know how much they can spend every month regardless of what the market does. Fixed-income investing is quite boring—continuously getting the same income month after month without ever having to invade your principal. But when the market does crash, fixed income becomes exciting because our client's income will be safe, just like it was in 2008. And they will keep getting their income month after month while leaving their principal alone. And all of us can sleep well as a result.

Most people have never expended the energy to develop a financial plan. They spend more time setting up a two-week vacation than they do sitting down with a professional financial advisor and putting together a comprehensive financial road map. Why? Because we have become a society of instant gratification, and we live for the moment. We want to be in the now. We don't want to consider the possibility that we are going to wake up one day eighty-five and broke. Or that the stock market might take another tumble. So most people never plan at all, and if you fail to plan, then you plan to fail.

Running out of money doesn't happen overnight; it's more like a slow-growing cancer that will eventually invade your body if you live long enough. Have you ever been driving, only to look down at your gauges and realize you're almost out of gas? Sure, everyone's done that. You get nervous and jittery and start crossing your fingers, hoping to make it to the next gas station. You may decide to conserve fuel by turning off the air or slowing down. If you're really low, and that red light is on, you may even start to panic. Your heart rate may go up a notch. Spending down your principal in retirement is kind of like that. It's not about the day you run out of money; it's about the journey. It makes you nervous that you are dipping into your principal month after month to pay the bills, hoping that the market doesn't turn south and you don't run out of gas before your life ends. Spending down your principal to pay the bills every month creates anxiety. What if you have another fifteen or twenty years left in the tank? It's not like you are going to wake up one morning and discover that you are down to the last ten bucks in your purse or your wallet. You'll start thinking about all of the things you can do to conserve fuel long before that point. Maybe it's time to stop playing golf. Maybe

I shouldn't travel for leisure or to see the grandchildren as much. Probably not the retirement you dreamed of.

However, all that nervousness and anxiety can be avoided if you have a financial plan in place. I like to tell people to think of their financial plan as Google Maps for their retirement. You can get directions from California to Florida on Google Maps. You can print it all out so that you know every turn you are going to take on which highway and how many miles each segment of the trip is going to be; but it can't let you know 100 percent of everything that's going to happen on the trip.

You may find that there is a major accident ahead, which forces you to take a detour. A road you were going to take might be flooded out and you have to find an alternative route. It's the same on your retirement journey. You're going to get to roads that are closed, and you are going to need a contingency plan. Everything is not going to go hunky-dory.

Then let's plan for that too. There's going to be monetary issues. There's going to be tax increases. There's going to be inflationary things, which we are already starting to see. There's going to be health issues that you can't know.

A financial plan allows you to look at that stuff ahead of time, set a benchmark for the future, and adjust when necessary. I'm a moderately terrible golfer, but I love to golf. If I break a hundred, I'm happy. Financial planning is a lot like golf. I envision myself on the tee box looking, you know, three hundred yards down the fairway, knowing I'm never going to get there because my drives are probably two and a quarter. I'm a big guy. I should be driving a lot further than that, but my mechanics are terrible.

Often I'm off by two or three degrees. And if you're off by two or three degrees on a two- or three-hundred-yard drive, you're going to be digging through the bushes. You're going to break a window. I've done that. You can't be off by that much and get away with it; but imagine that immediately after driving the ball, the ball gets out fifty yards, and you realize your drive is not headed in the desired direction. Suddenly, you snap your fingers, and the ball instantaneously stops midflight and levitates in midair. You fly out there, like in a video game, and move the ball back to where it's supposed to be. How often would you hit your target? Every time!

That's a great dream I've often wished would come true.

The bad news is you can't do that in golf. The good news is you *can* do that with a financial plan. When you're sixty-five or seventy, on the tee box of the rest of your life with potentially another thirty years to go, you can't be off by two degrees every year. You'll run out of money. But if you're off by two degrees and you have a review with your financial advisor every year or two, you can bring that ball back in line so you don't ever wake up one day and wonder, "Oh my gosh. Why am I out of money?" You can make those minor adjustments along the way.

Your financial plan is your guidebook to your retirement, but it is not written in stone. It needs to be periodically revisited. Life is fluid. Circumstances change. Your interests might change. You might suddenly develop an interest in Incan archaeology and want to visit Machu Picchu in Peru when you retire. Your plan must be fluid enough to allow you to do the things in the future you may not even realize you want to do.

You also need a plan B. You cannot always depend upon Google Maps to get you where you are going. Yes, Google uses a powerful algorithm to calculate the best route from point A to point B, but it only works perfectly every time in a static environment. Life is not static. It is dynamic, and things have a way of coming out of left field at the most inopportune time. COVID is a perfect example that no one saw coming. It won't be the last. The unfortunate reality is that a financial plan is one of those things that you didn't know you needed until it was too late. If you don't have a road map to help you navigate through your golden years, you might find yourself lost in the barren wilderness of old age with every day more boring, more hopeless than the one before, sitting alone in the waiting room of life, all because you did not plan.

Your financial plan is your guidebook to your retirement, but it is not written in stone. It needs to be periodically revisited.

A well-thought-out financial plan takes all these factors into account: taxes, inflation, interest rates, when to take Social Security, when and how to take your pension, and the best way for you to protect your nest egg while still getting the income from it that you need. Your financial plan includes having a budget for things like long-term care. It has a contingency plan for what happens when one spouse dies. It spells out your wishes when both spouses die. What goes where? Who gets what and how much? It takes a lot of effort and expertise to get all the details just right for you. Everything is customized. This is one time when one size does not fit all.

CHAPTER THREE

What You Need to Know about Picking a Financial Advisor

WHAT IS A "financial advisor"? The most common definition is that a financial advisor is a professional who offers financial services designed to develop, improve, or protect their client's financial situation. To offer those services and advise about those services, the advisor has to complete specific training and hold specific licenses.

The Financial Industry Regulatory Authority (FINRA) has developed regulations to determine who may use the term *financial advisor*. These include licensed securities brokers, investment advisors, private bankers, accountants, lawyers, insurance agents, and financial planners.

But once a candidate complies, they can hold themselves out as a financial advisor. Although there are some minimum educational requirements that they must adhere to, there is no requirement for an advisor to get any type of advanced education, like qualifying to become a Certified Financial Planner (CFP) or Chartered Financial

Consultant (ChFC). To become a CFP, one must hold a bachelor's degree, complete a Certified Financial Planner Board of Standards Inc. (CFP Board) registered course of study, gain three years of experience as a financial advisor, and pass a certification exam. To maintain CFP status, the advisor has to complete thirty hours of continuing education every year. Because of the extra effort, only 20 percent of financial advisors are CFPs.

I've completed the requirements to be credentialed as a Chartered Financial Consultant (ChFC). This designation is even more elevated and requires the holder to complete more courses than the CFP.[10] These include three years of full-time, industry-related business experience and the completion of nine college-level courses equivalent to twenty-seven semester credit hours. Candidates must prove mastery of more than one hundred topics pertaining to advanced financial planning, such as the following:

- Financial Planning: Process and Environment

- Insurance Planning

- Employee Benefits Planning

- Income Tax Planning

- Estate Tax, Gift Tax, and Transfer Tax Planning

- Asset Protection Planning

- Retirement Planning

- Estate Planning

- Applications of Comprehensive Financial Planning

I personally believe the CFP credential should be the entry-level

---

10   SmartAsset, "What's the Difference Between a CFP and a CHFC?," January 14, 2022, https://smartasset.com/retirement/chfc-vs-cfp-whats-the-difference.

designation that every advisor should have before they are qualified to manage a client's retirement. But I also believe that more education is better than less and that any advisor who is serious about helping you and acting in your best interest should also obtain the ChFC, which is why I did so. At a minimum, I highly suggest working with an advisor who at least holds the CFP designation.

There is a significant difference from one financial advisor to another. You can generally break the world of financial advisors down into three categories. You can act as your own financial advisor. You can work with a large multinational firm. Or you can engage the services of a Registered Investment Advisor (RIA) who either owns or works for an independent firm. Let's explore the differences.

Hiring Yourself

If you do not have a financial advisor, and have hired yourself for the job, there are some good tools that provide the education and research you need to make informed decisions. But there is a difference between being a do-it-yourself investor and being a gambler.

If you are financially literate and willing to put in the elbow grease to get the knowledge you need to make informed decisions, and you have the inner fortitude to stick with your plan, then you may correctly classify yourself as an investor. If you don't know much about investments and economics and have simply checked a few boxes, by which you have chosen your investments, then you may be classified as a gambler. Hoping and wishing that your investments go up in value, without knowing anything about them, is a rocky risk. Everyone who has ever sat down at a Las Vegas slot machine did so with the *hope* that they were going to win. They cross their fingers and toes while spinning the reels time after time with absolutely no control or certainty of the outcome. If you cannot articulate why you own the investments you do, and you've just been hanging on to them for years hoping to win, you're doing the same thing as gambling. If you're set on doing it yourself, though, there are several types of firms whose services you may want to utilize along the way.

Discount Brokers

Discount brokers are good for investors who know what they are doing and who want to do their own investing. I've been known to say that if you know what you're doing regarding any task, and if you want to take time out of your life to do that task, then you don't need a professional. For example, if you know how to change your own brakes and you want to do so, then don't bother hiring a mechanic. If your toilet begins leaking and you know how to change the ring seal, you have to decide the worth of your time. You are going to have to shut off the water, drain the water in the toilet, lift off the existing toilet, replace the ring seal, and reinstall the toilet. If you know how to do all of this and you're willing to take the time to do the repair, then you don't need a plumber.

If you have a good working knowledge about investments and the time to spend on them, then you don't need an investment advisor. Just keep in mind, the more important the task, the more you should consider hiring a professional to help you. If you mess up changing a toilet, the worst-case scenario is a puddle of dirty water—and then you call the plumber. This is not a huge risk. If you mess up on your brake job, the worst-case scenario is you have an auto accident and you could die. The risk is much greater here. If you mess up on your investments, the worst-case scenario is you run out of money before you run out of life. That is the risk in hiring yourself, and it's a big one. Unless you can demonstrate solid investment expertise, I don't recommend you hire yourself for the job. If you make a mistake, you may not be able to go back and fix it.

When you hire a discount broker, you are technically choosing to manage your investments yourself. The broker probably has an 800 number to call and ask general questions about your investments, but they aren't privy to the rest of your assets. Since they are not financial advisors in the true sense of the word, they cannot coordinate an overall strategy for you. They are only aware of the account you have with them. Because you won't have a dedicated advisor assigned to your case, you'll get someone new every time you call for advice. Most discount brokers are not licensed to give financial planning advice, nor do they have the expertise to help you put all your puzzle pieces in the right place. Simply stated, you are the quarterback, and the discount broker is one of the cheerleaders urging you onward.

Robo-Advisors

In this age of artificial intelligence, the investment world has come up with the term *robo-advisor*. While the name makes it sound modern and convenient, it is really nothing more than a remake of models that have been used in portfolios for decades. A model refers to your investments getting matched to a particular strategy, much in the same way that is offered to everyone else. Most large firms will categorize you into one of six or eight strategies, and your portfolio will get put into whatever investments that strategy includes. It is similar to a mutual fund where you get the same investments as everyone else who is invested in it. The difference is that you get to enjoy the illusion of actually picking investments and creating a "custom" portfolio. It is, of course, only customized in the sense that you assemble your portfolio from the prescreened choices that have been offered.

The sophistication of models has increased right alongside the growth of computers and software. Robo-advisors appeal to average retail investors because of their lower fees. Some of the robo-advisors have very sophisticated algorithms and ask a lot of questions, making a customer feel as if they are getting more comprehensive advice than they would in a model portfolio. At the end of the day, you're still in a model that doesn't know anything about you other than how you've answered a particular set of generalized questions. There is danger in this because the robo-advisor model cannot offer an opinion. If you tell the model that you are super aggressive, and you want all of your money in stocks, the robo-advisor is not going to argue with you. It's not going to say, "What? Are you nuts? You're seventy-five years old and can lose half of your value if the market has a repeat of 2008. Are you prepared to go back to work if your portfolio plummets by 50 percent?" When you stop and think about it, a robo-advisor can turn your golden years into a dusty, rusty wasteland, all for the sake of convenience.

An example I often use has to do with the medical field. There are people who have medical conditions and are diagnosing themselves based on information they are getting from the internet. Not a good idea. There is no replacement for a doctor who knows you, can collect meaningful data, and has the training and expertise to properly diagnose your problem and devise a treatment plan. Likewise, there is no replacement for an investment advisor or financial planner who knows you and understands the array of options available to get you the results you need.

At the end of the day, regardless of whether you have your retirement nest egg at a discount brokerage firm or it is being managed by a robo-advisor, you are still doing it yourself. And if you make only one mistake, the results can be disastrous. We just took on a new client who had $250,000 in his retirement account. A year earlier, it was worth $280,000. He invested (gambled) in something that sounded good, but he ended up losing $30,000 last year! And stocks went up over 30 percent during that time. Fortunately, this didn't cost him his retirement, but he could have used that cash for the car he wanted. This is truly a case of what you don't know can hurt you. You better make sure you know what you're doing if you are going to go this route.

What if you've decided that you don't want to blaze these financial trails on your own? What are your other options? You can hire an advisor, who generally works as a broker for a large Wall Street firm or as an independent Registered Investment Advisor (RIA).

Brokers

Most new advisors who break into the Wall Street world do so by cutting their teeth at a big global firm that shows them the ropes. In the world of Wall Street, the ropes are mutual funds, which are the primary product that these big full-service broker-dealers, also known as "wirehouses," sell. If you work for one of these firms, you are generally expected to sell mutual funds. Therefore, I often view "advisors" as glorified salespeople. If you want to know whether your advisor is a salesperson or a true advisor, ask them to help you develop a financial plan like we just discussed. You'll find out very quickly which title they fall under.

If a licensed operator on the other end of the phone line suggests investing in mutual funds, it's easy to believe that, out of all the investments that are available, this representative is recommending what is best for you. Hmm. No. Mutual funds are what brokers sell, and that's why they're recommending them. There's a reason stockbrokers are called stockbrokers. When they sell prepackaged stocks in a mutual fund, they earn a residual commission every time they sell one.

Imagine that you needed a truck to haul some dirt, and you went to a Porsche dealership. Would you be surprised when the salesperson tries to sell you an overpriced sports car? Of course not, because that's what the dealership sells. It doesn't matter that you don't need a Porsche. If they don't sell one to you, they don't make any money. You would never walk into a Porsche dealership looking for a pickup truck, because you know that they don't sell pickups.

The problem with the big Wall Street firms, though, is that what they sell is not transparent. Most people believe that these firms sell financial advice, that their salespeople are financial advisors. Most people are unaware that the stockbrokers at these firms want to sell you mutual funds. There may be another investment that is better suited for you; however, it's not sold by this firm, which is why you don't hear about other options. Without knowing it, you could be sucked into an aggressive investment strategy that's not in your best interest. And by the time you realize it, it may be too late.

Most stockbrokers tend to be aggressive by nature. Imagine this: If a high school grad met with her guidance counselor and described herself as being a little bit shy, she doesn't like to take risks, and sales are not her thing, would that guidance counselor ever recommend that she become a stockbroker? Probably not. This is why I say stockbrokers tend to be type A personalities and aggressive by nature. It's only the more aggressive-natured folks who tend to gravitate toward a career that involves a certain level of risk. And the firm's job is to perpetuate that aggressiveness and turn that stockbroker into a superstar salesperson.

This is where you must be really aware of your personal investment philosophy and your risk tolerance. There are salespeople out there who will put you into whatever mutual funds are currently showing returns that suggest you could double or triple your funds and retire in luxury. Salespeople are not typically fiduciaries, and they are being paid a commission to recommend these products.

I want to take you into a stockbroker's world. I believe that if you have a surface-level understanding of how the securities industry works, you'll be armed to make the best decision for yourself. You can't make a good decision with bad information. They call this "garbage in, garbage out."

If you're a new advisor in the financial services industry, the first thing you have to do is get customers. To get new customers, you have to sell them something. That is probably why most financial advisors enter the industry as "brokers" for a big firm. I believe it's the easiest way to start getting customers.

As a broker at a firm, you make a commission every time you sell a product (mutual fund), and when you sell a mutual fund, you continue to get a residual commission for as long as the buyer remains a customer. This is what is referred to as building a book of business. Products that you have sold will continue to pay you time and again until your customer dies or transfers his or her money elsewhere.

These multinational firms spend lots of money on marketing.

They have expensive, cinematic commercials that emphasize their solid reputations built upon decades of experience and longevity as a firm. This is all designed to make it possible for you, the junior "broker," to sit in the cubicle farm and take phone calls. Once you acquire more experience and a few clients, management may give you a list of clients who are in need of a new broker. Your job is to call them so you can sell them something else.

If you want to be a salesperson, it's a pretty easy way to make a decent amount of money. Churn your way through the list and salvage as many new or returning customers as you can, talk them into letting you manage their accounts, and collect your commissions by moving other customers' money around based upon the recommendations of the firm's analysts. All you have to do is show up at eight, make phone calls, check a few boxes every time you sell something, and leave at five. The only requirement is that you make money for the firm. If you make money for the client as well, that's just a bonus. You'll probably never make as much money as an independent financial advisor, because you're not really a financial advisor. You're a salesperson. You don't have a fiduciary responsibility to a client like an independent financial advisor does. You are just peddling the firm's advice to the trusting, uninformed public, and it's simply a numbers game.

When you choose a firm to work for, your loyalty is to that firm, not the clients. This is a fact most investors are unaware of. You must sell the products that the firm offers. And if a firm doesn't offer a particular product, then you can't sell it, even if you know deep down inside that the other product may be a better option for your customer. You can't pay your mortgage if you recommend investments that your firm doesn't sell.

If you don't like one firm, there's always an opportunity at another firm. If all you want is a sales job where you make decent money, and you are fairly smart, ethical, and reliable, then being a salesperson for a big firm is not a bad career. Just don't get personally involved with the customers and keep it all about the numbers. Don't worry about the retired schoolteacher who calls with a question about her account and discovers that another, less experienced broker has taken over her account because you've been promoted, or you've moved on to another firm. You sold her the mutual fund that the firm's analysts recommended. Her new broker will tell her that he or she appreciates her frustration or even her anger, but she just needs to stick to the buy-and-hold strategy that you initially told her about. This is the same advice that all brokers disseminate. Buy and hold is their mantra.

In the meantime, you've moved on to another list of customers. It's just the way the financial advisor business works. As long as you're making money, nothing else matters, right? To paraphrase P. T. Barnum, "There is a customer born every minute." For many, that is sadly true; but it isn't that way for all advisors.

I understand this because I was once in that role at a brokerage firm. I hated it, because I didn't want to be a salesperson. I wanted to be an advisor. I did not want to be pigeonholed into selling clients stuff that was in the firm's best interest, and I actually wanted to help my clients do what was best for them. I knew there were other investments available that were better suited for their phase of life; however, I wasn't permitted to discuss them because the firm didn't sell them.

As a broker at a large firm, you do not have a fiduciary standard to act in the client's best interest. You must act in the firm's best interest, and specifically in the interests of the shareholders. And the more mutual funds you sell, the better the shareholders do. That is why I truly believe that most advisors who work with a large firm are essentially salespeople disguised as advisors. Unfortunately, many advisors don't even recognize this.

Does this mean that there is no place for commissioned stockbrokers? Of course not. But you must understand their role as salespeople and why they are making the recommendations they are making.

Working for a bank is similar. If you are a new advisor looking for a place to park your license, and you feel that working for one of these large firms is a little too daunting, getting hired by a bank as their advisor may be a better fit. An advisor who starts at the bank is sitting at the desk, studying the bank's approved investment products. Banks are often contracted with a very limited number and type of investments, so they are not doing their customers any favors. The advisor's job is to sell those investments.

You don't make a ton of money, but you don't have to do a lot of work. You show up, sit at your desk, and wait for the tellers to find out that someone's CD has matured. That teller sends the customer over to you, the bank's "financial advisor." Because interest rates on CDs are so low, a lot of investors are transferring their accounts to other investments with more upside potential. The bank wants to keep that money in the bank, so you just got a free client. You advise the investors that they will save money by transferring the funds into one of the bank's investment vehicles, since the bank has already preapproved their existing customer. And you have to show them how they are going to get a higher rate of return than they received with the CD. It's certainly convenient for the customer. You just facilitate the transfer paperwork with a confident smile and a professional handshake, hoping that they don't ask you too many questions. It's like shooting fish in a barrel. You show up at eight or whatever time the bank opens, and you leave when the bank closes, and that's the extent of your responsibility. Many advisors who start working for the banks and big firms stay there for years, because it can be a cushy job if you have the right amount of salesmanship. And there's not a lot of responsibility.

Once you know what goes on backstage, you really have to stretch your imagination to find any major pros of working with a bank advisor or a large brokerage firm. If you're into name recognition, working with them would be a pro, because these firms spend billions on ads. A lot of people like the fact that (they think) these firms are secure; in fact, they even call them *secur*ities. Sounds safe, right? Ironically securities are very insecure.

But there is a positive shift occurring in the financial advisory world. Many salespeople have begun to wake up to the cold reality that they are just that, salespeople. They have come to a moral crossroads in their life. They truly want to be advisors, advocates for you, but they're beginning to realize that they can't do that if they're pushing products for a conglomerate. As a result, there is a wave of salespeople transitioning into the RIA world so they can act as true advisors, not salespeople.

The reason I call it a moral crossroads is the same reason that led me to become an RIA. It is about why individuals get into finance and what they are trying to accomplish. Are they playing the short game, or are they in it for the long haul? Are they making a paycheck, or are they building a career? Are they selling customers suitable mutual funds, or are they truly advising their clients on how to build their wealth? The moral choice, in my opinion, is becoming a fiduciary and taking the long view toward your client's best interests.

Registered Investment Advisor (RIA)

A Registered Investment Advisor is a fee-only advisor. In 2020, there were 13,494 RIAs working in the United States, up from 10,511 in 2012.[11] That's a 28 percent increase in just eight short years. These advisors are either registered with the US Securities and Exchange Commission or a securities administrator of the state in which they practice. RIAs must know you and fully understand your vision and your financial goals, because the law requires

> *The moral choice, in my opinion, is becoming a fiduciary and taking the long view toward your client's best interests.*

---

11 Statista, "Number of Registered Investment Advisors (RIAs) Employed in the United States from 2012 to 2020," April 15, 2021, https://www.statista.com/statistics/614815/number-of-rias-employed-usa/.

them to cater to your best interests. Your investments are just one piece of your retirement puzzle. A bank advisor, big-firm salesperson, discount broker, or robo-advisor is not capable of helping you put the rest of the puzzle together the same way an investment advisor is.

Independent RIA firms have a fiduciary standard, which is significantly different than what other firms or brokers require. A fiduciary is a person to whom property or power is entrusted for the benefit of another. That means that everything that is done on your behalf must be done based upon what is in your best interest, not mine. That even includes when I tell the custodian to execute trades. They must be done under a "best execution" standard, meaning they must strive to trade securities with the best combination of low cost and best timing. My duty of loyalty and due care makes me put your best interests above mine, even if it costs me. I must give you accurate advice and thorough analysis and avoid any appearance of a conflict of interest.

Brokers at big firms do not have a fiduciary standard, which means that they do not have to act in your best interest. When you work directly with a broker at one of these firms, you are operating on their retail platform designed just for you, the retail customer. And their legal standard is one of suitability. As long as the investment is suitable for you, they can recommend it, and if it is discovered that there are other investments that would've worked better, they will be exonerated. If a broker at the big firm has ten mutual funds that are all suitable but pay different commissions, they can sell you the one with the largest commission under the suitability standard, even if the other nine are better suited for you. If the fund tanks and you attempt to sue him for not recommending another one of the ten that didn't fail, you will lose that case in court. As long as the one he sold you was suitable at the time he sold it to you, you lose.

On the other hand, if you made an investment based upon a recommendation from an RIA, and you can prove that there was one better recommendation that the advisor could've made on your behalf, then they would lose the case. I have to investigate the investments as thoroughly for you as I would for myself. That is why the big firm has "customers," whereas I have "clients." It is a subtle but very important distinction.

The good news is that, even when you work with an RIA, your money is still going to be housed with one of those large firms, just not on the retail side. Most of these firms have a retail component and an institutional platform. When you work with an RIA who is independent like I am, your investments will be held on the institutional platform with whatever firm the RIA has decided to use. This allows RIAs to use these firms as the custodians for their clients. The RIA does not hold the investments; rather, the investments are held by the custodian. If you ever want to fire your RIA, you can simply call the custodian and revoke the RIA's authority to trade on your behalf. Because your investments are held by the custodian, the RIA only has authority to manage them. And if you want to revoke that authority, you can do so at will.

Working with an RIA gives you the best of both worlds. Your money is held at a large institution, but you still have a relationship with a fiduciary advisor who is looking out for your best interests. When you hire us, your accounts get transferred to the custodian with whom we work. Your money is not being commingled with my bank account or my company's bank account. Most people are very appreciative of this, because it gives them the confidence of having personal attention from an advisor but still having access to the array of products offered by the big firm.

The custodian we have chosen to work with is TD Ameritrade. Charles Schwab has purchased TD Ameritrade, and we've been told that the consolidated firm will keep the Charles Schwab name. Whether that comes to fruition or not remains to be seen. Either way, it doesn't matter for us, or you, because we don't work for either of them; they provide us timely and direct access to the market and sophisticated investment tools. They handle the accounting and record keeping, and it is their responsibility to send you monthly statements. An RIA is independent and does not work for the custodian. Some advisors work for an RIA, and some advisors own the RIA. I've chosen to own mine, because it gives me greater control and authority to do what is best for my clients. It also gives me greater responsibility.

When you come to an independent RIA like Providence Financial & Insurance Services (www.providencefinancialinc.com), you have an advisor who is educated, trained, and licensed to talk with you about your current financial status and what resources you have available. This advisor will do their best to accommodate your financial literacy and your financial goals. We then put together a financial strategy that takes you from where you are and sets you on a path to where you want to be. We commit to a relationship with you that is built upon honesty, respect, and integrity. We are going to find out what you know and educate you on what you do not know. We will explain every part of the process so that you understand what we are doing and why we are doing it. We collaborate as partners to find the right path up the mountain.

One of the many differences between me and an advisor at a big brokerage firm is that I'm here to stay. Big-firm advisors are known for moving often and following the money; I am here because I care about your future, and I have a natural passion for helping others.

I often use the example of H&R Block. You probably know that they are a global firm that does taxes for their customers. I used to own a tax firm for nine years, so I understand how that game works. The required training program at H&R Block is extremely basic, and the average starting wage is $12.50 per hour.[12] Are you going to trust them to do your taxes? If you have no money, and your only source of income is derived from Social Security, that's fine; all you need is an order taker, and that's what they are. If your tax return is even slightly more complicated than that, do you really want someone who took a two-week tax course?[13] Why would you hire them? My guess is because of one thing: name recognition. Everyone's heard of them, so they must be good, right?

There are a lot of independent CPAs who own their own firms. Some of them have grown their firms to large levels, and some of them have decided to remain as small mom-and-pop shops. But there is one thing that they have that H&R Block does not have: a vested interest in you. It is their business, and you are not just a number; you are a client. And that's a huge differentiator.

My clients are my clients, and I fight for them. I do everything in my power to make sure I learn my clients' goals and help them achieve them, because they are not just numbers to me. They are in my care, and I owe it to them to continuously improve my knowledge of the different investment vehicles, the markets, the economy, and the regulations that govern the financial industry. When 5:00 p.m. comes around, I don't just go home and wait for the next day to show up to work again. This is not just a job for me. During my "off" hours, I read and research and continue learning so that I can better serve my existing clients. Why? Because I have a vested interest in them. I can't just put in my resignation if I decide I want an easier route.

---

12   PayScale, "Average Hourly Rate for H&R Block Employees," https://www.payscale.com/research/US/Employer=H%26R_Block/Hourly_Rate.

13   H&R Block, "How to Become a Tax Preparer," July 13, 2017, https://www.hrblock.com/tax-center/around-block/become-tax-preparer/.

When I'm doing research, I'm not trying to pigeonhole my client into a product that I am supposed to sell, and I'm not limited to an analyst's recommendations. I'm not trying to figure out which mutual fund is going to give me the best commission. If I advise someone to invest in a mutual fund, I will tell them why it's the best vehicle for meeting their investment goals.

I have access to all the investments. My team investigates which investment or combination of investments is best for your investment vision. I'm not trying to sell you mutual funds, but if a mutual fund is right for you, I have access to nearly all the same funds that the brokers do. If mutual funds are not right for you, I can recommend other things that are. It all boils down to what we discuss in our first consultation, and I determine that by asking the following questions:

- What do you want your money to do for you?

- What are your investment goals and why?

- What assets do you have to work with?

- Are your current strategies supporting or conflicting your goals and philosophies?

- Are you invested properly for your phase of life, or should you be thinking about making a change?

By obtaining answers to these five questions, I can successfully execute a plan designed specifically for you.

I have a nine-year-old son, Aiden, and a five-year-old daughter, Audria. When my wife, Anca, and I found out we were pregnant the first time around, I decided to use my evening hours to get my law degree and become an attorney. Most of my advisor friends find this incredulous, because I already make a good living. When I announced years ago to my friends and family that I was going to become an attorney, their facial expressions contorted as if they had just sucked on a lemon. They couldn't understand why. To them it seemed like more unnecessary work.

A primary reason, though, is because I also own a law firm and assist my clients in setting up their estate plans. What good is setting up a perfect financial plan while you're alive if a good chunk is going to be gobbled up by the court system via probate or go to the Internal Revenue Service through taxes? If you have not done any estate planning, then Uncle Sam may be a beneficiary of your estate, and you may not even know it. No comprehensive financial plan would be complete without a properly drafted and implemented estate plan. Even when you're gone, the nest egg that you leave behind is still money that you've sacrificed for. If it is just going to get wasted on needless expenses and taxes after you depart from this planet, wouldn't you be better off spending it now? At least you'll get something for it. I became an attorney to serve my clients even better with their estate planning.

The choice here is simple: Would you rather have an advisor who has limited products and gets paid commission every time you agree with his recommendation? Or would you rather have an advisor who has access to all the investments and gets paid the same fee regardless of what he or she suggests? If the former, then the big Wall Street brokers are your best bet. If the latter, then you should search for a Registered Investment Advisor you can trust.

Are you starting to get a feel for the difference between those who work for a large firm as compared to those who own their own firm? My firm is my baby. I live by a phrase that I heard many years ago that says, "If you love what you do, you'll never work a day in your life." I thank the Lord every day that I am not working. I haven't worked eight to five in twenty years. Twelve-hour days are not uncommon, but it never feels like work. Imagine getting paid to do what you love. Yes, I look forward to Fridays. But I also look forward to Mondays. I have an extensive list of very happy, very loyal clients who refer me to their friends and family without hesitation because I have helped them realize their financial goals and retire without ever having to worry about running out of money. For that, I have been blessed in a multitude of ways. I love what I do. It is not my job; it is my calling. I get paid to help others accomplish their goals, and by doing so, I am accomplishing mine.

What Questions Should You Ask?

I've spent some time in this chapter talking about my philosophies and how I work, because I can't speak for other advisors. I can only speak for how I run my business and how I feel about my profession. But there are many great Registered Investment Advisors available to you, many of whom I am privileged to be friends with. Some of them are probably right in your backyard. I suggest you find one to help you.

> *It is not my job; it is my calling. I get paid to help others accomplish their goals, and by doing so, I am accomplishing mine.*

If you're going to hire an investment advisor, there are a few questions that you should ask to find the right fit. And I want to give you a sample so you can be prepared when you talk to them.

The first question should always be about the advisor's education, training, and experience. In a perfect world, a financial advisor would have an undergraduate degree in finance, economics, accounting, or some field of study related to the business. At a minimum, I believe that any advisor you are considering should have their CFP designation or the ChFC designation, as I have. And if he or she has a bachelor's in finance or, in my case, a law degree, that's a bonus.

Ask advisors where they received their training. What firms they have worked for. How long they worked there. Ask about their basic investment philosophy. They should be able to not only tell you what to invest in but also "why" you are invested in a particular investment. Their philosophy should be supportive of your investing goals.

If you're in your retirement years, ask them how they intend for you to get the cash you need monthly from your portfolio. If they tell you that they are going to sell shares periodically to get you your income, as opposed to developing a plan that will allow you to live off your interest and dividends, you should run away for reasons that will be discussed later in this book. They should be able to articulate the reasons why they are recommending a certain strategy. And if they can't, that is a red flag. Ask as many questions as necessary until you understand how they are going to invest your money.

Don't be afraid to dig deep. A true advisor will love that. But many so-called advisors hide behind a wall of confusion. Confused clients don't ask a lot of questions, because they typically don't know what to ask. If you just blindly follow an advisor's advice, you may get hurt. If you leave their office or hang up the phone and you don't understand what they just told you, be cautious. I would encourage you to keep searching.

Finally, how long have they been an independent financial advisor? I have been a financial advisor for over twenty-two years, and I can tell you that if an advisor has not been in the industry for at least half that time, then there are things that they don't know. Don't let them use your nest egg to learn. If an advisor has been in the business for a decade or less, they only know of the good times.

They did not live through the 2008 crash. And they certainly did not experience the dot-com crash of 2001.

There's nothing that can replace experience. I often joke that experience is something you get ... right after you needed it. Unfortunately for advisors, experience takes a long time to get. If you are contemplating building a long-term relationship with an advisor, you need to have confidence that he or she knows what they are doing and will be there when economic conditions start to turn and your financial plan needs to be recalibrated.

CHAPTER FOUR

What You Don't Know about the Different Asset Classes

Aren't Stocks The Best Way To Accumulate Wealth?

WE'RE TOLD THAT the way to get rich is to invest in the stock market. Buy low and sell high is the path to financial freedom. Wall Street would have you think this is the silver bullet for everyone all the time. Many have fallen into the trap of believing this. However, stocks are just one of three major asset classes. The other two are fixed income and cash. Most people have not taken the time to educate themselves on each asset class. They don't know the differences between them, how they work together, and what risks are involved in each one.

Let's start with stocks. Each share of stock represents a percentage of ownership in a company.

When listening to the daily news, we are indoctrinated with the numbers from the Dow Jones Industrial Average (DJIA), as this is likely the most commonly discussed valuation of the market. Very few people outside the financial world really know what those numbers represent. The DJIA is a stock market index that represents the value of thirty large, publicly owned global companies. This index was first calculated on May 26, 1896, by Dow Jones & Company cofounders Charles Dow and Edward Jones.[14] These thirty companies represent the various sectors of the general economy, and the value of the Dow is supposed to represent the value of the companies inside of it. As with any index, its performance is influenced by corporate and economic reports, as well as political events and natural disasters that investors believe could harm the economy.

But that's not the only index. There are dozens of other indexes that sample a larger number of companies. The S&P 500 is considered a more reliable index than the Dow because it measures the performance of more than five hundred large-cap companies that are traded on US stock exchanges. There are even indexes for specific sectors of the market. They are all efforts to make rational and objective determinations about the health and direction of the global economy, something that is often irrational and reactionary to any number of factors.

Before you make a knowledgeable investment in a particular stock, you need to read financial news reports about the company, digest the target company's financial reports, and compare and analyze the P/E ratio, sales growth, earnings per share, and many other variables. Most people who don't work in the financial industry find it overwhelming and confusing and don't even know where to start. That's why they turn to mutual funds.

A mutual fund is a pool of investments in a wide range of securities. When you invest in a mutual fund, you are purchasing a propor-

---

14   Investopedia, "When Was the Dow Jones Industrial Average Created?," March 18, 2021, https://www.investopedia.com/ask/answers/100214/when-did-dow-jones-industrial-average-djia-begin.asp.

tionate share of the investments that are in the fund as well as sharing in the fund's performance, either positive or negative. They are formed by a professional money manager who collects a pool of money from investors and allocates those funds into different investments. The advantages to the individual investor are access to professional management, diversification, and ease of liquidity. The disadvantages are that there are operating costs, fees, and lack of transparency. If you don't know much about investments and are in the accumulation phase of life, with many years ahead of you, mutual funds are a great way to dollar cost average into the market. But you must have your eyes open and learn as much about the fund as possible before you put your money into it.

Should you just blindly put all your money into the stock market, though, even if you have many years ahead? Wall Street will likely answer that question in the affirmative, because they sell stocks. They want you to believe that no matter where we are at any point in time, you should buy stocks and hold on to them forever. This is the solution to everything. Just hang in there and keep buying stocks, and you'll be fine. Is that true? Let's analyze the history of the stock market and find out. I've had this conversation with thousands of people over my career, and they're always amazed by what they learn. You will be too.

History tends to repeat itself over the long run. There are a lot of reasons for that. History is made up of generations after generations. When you boil it down, history is just a bunch of kids making the same mistakes that their parents made. Do your kids listen to you the first time you tell them something? Daddy did this, so don't do that. Does that ever work?

History is just a bunch of grown-up children making the same mistakes over and over again and trying to learn from them. It's a vicious cycle. History absolutely repeats itself, but Wall Street doesn't want you to believe that. They want you to believe that the market is random. History tells a different story.

We now have over two hundred years of solid stock market data. When you study that data, you begin to realize that there are actually predictable and repeatable trends. Not monthly, not yearly, but over the long run. Generally speaking, two hundred years of solid history tells us that if you invest in stocks over a thirty-to-thirty-five-year time period, you'll probably average somewhere in the range of 8 to 9 percent per year of growth plus dividends—which should bring you up to the 9 or 10 percent range.

DOW JONES INDUSTRIAL AVERAGE DJIA SINCE 1900

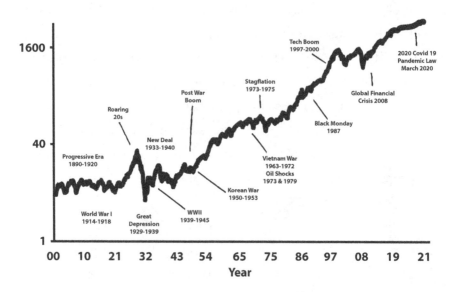

CHART B
Source: Advisors' Academy

However, every thirty-to-thirty-five-year period is subdivided into a couple distinct periods. There are often periods that last a decade or more, like the nineties, or the last decade, where the market has strong double-digit returns. However, these bull markets are always followed by flat periods. And when I say flat, I don't mean flat as in a straight line. I'm referring to periods of time that last as long as ten or twenty years when the market has ups and downs that wash each other out, resulting in absolutely no growth. Allow me to discuss the most recent thirty-four years of stock market history so you can see how history generally plays out.

GSPC YAHOO FINANCE CHART

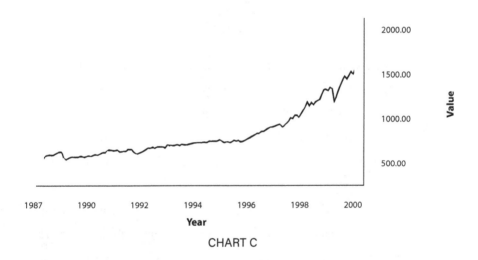

CHART C

If you look at the thirteen-year period starting thirty-four years ago, from 1987 through 2000, you'll discover that the S&P 500 Index rose from 230 to the 1500 range. That's strong double-digit growth of roughly 15.5 percent per year for thirteen years. But how did the market do during the next thirteen years, from 2000 to 2013? It was absolutely flat! The S&P 500 was at 1517 in September 2000, and it was at 1514 in March 2013. No growth at all! What a contrast between two thirteen-year periods.

GSPC YAHOO FINANCE CHART

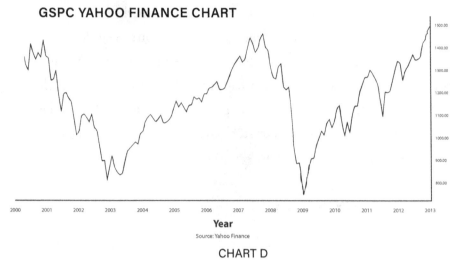

Source: Yahoo Finance

CHART D

As you study the chart, you'll notice that between 2000 and 2013, the market had two major drops and recoveries that washed each other out. On March 24, 2000, the S&P 500 Index hit a high of 1552. By October 10, 2002, the "Tech Crash" had siphoned off 51 percent of the market's value as the S&P 500 hit a low of 768. Stocks took five years to work their way back up to 1576 for a high on October 11, 2007. Then, just as everyone thought they were safe, the subprime debacle occurred and the mortgage bubble burst. The 2008 financial meltdown lopped 57 percent off the market as the S&P 500 bottomed out at 676 in March 2009. If you were invested in the market during this time, it would've taken nearly six years for your portfolio to get back to even. The end result? Two crashes and two recoveries between 2000 and 2013, providing exactly zero return to investors. What has the market done since 2013? The S&P 500 has grown from 1500 to over 4500 as of September 2021. That's over 14.5 percent annualized return!

In summary, during the thirteen-year period from 1987 through 2000, the S&P 500 had great growth. For the next thirteen-year period from 2000 through 2013, the S&P 500 had no growth. During the following eight-year period from 2013 through 2021, the market once again has had great growth. Are you starting to see a pattern?

Good periods are often followed by flat periods, just as has happened over the last thirty-four years. What would your return have been had you invested in the S&P 500 thirty-four years ago, assuming you just let your investment ride through 2021? The answer is 8.87 percent per year! Plus, you would have also received dividends that would probably put you close to 10 percent average return per year. Not bad. Market history tells us that you'll probably average 9–10 percent per year if you have a thirty-to-thirty-five-year time horizon. Anything shorter than that becomes a guessing game. From 1987 through 2000 and again from 2013 through 2021, you would have done well. But not from 2000 through 2013.

As you can see, there can be a significant difference from one period to another. As of September 2021, the S&P 500 was at 4500.

This is the highest it has ever been, which is likely driving you to ask the question, "Where do we go from here?" The answer: *who cares?*! If you study the previous charts, it may seem that our current bull market may be headed to an end. The stock market already had thirteen good years followed by thirteen bad years—and now followed by another thirteen good years, when considering that our current bull market began when the market bottomed out in March of 2009. If you go back even farther in history, you'll notice that this pattern is typical of a normal stock market. Good periods followed by bad periods. This is the way the market has worked for over two hundred years.

Here's what you need to understand, though. If you care where the market is going to go from here, it's a strong signal that you're not investing wisely. If you're in the accumulation phase of life and have thirty-plus years in front of you, do you care what the market does in the short run? You shouldn't. Because it doesn't matter. However, if you're planning on retiring in the next five years, and you have your entire portfolio invested in stocks, then of course you care. Because if the stock market goes against you, it may force you to delay retirement. You're invested wrong! You should never put yourself in a position where you can only retire if the stock market moves in your favor. That, my friends, is called gambling.

Just today, I spoke with an individual whose retirement nest egg is $2 million, with all of it invested in stock mutual funds. He is a seventy-one-year-old physician and plans on retiring in two years. At retirement, he'll need to take $75,000 per year from his portfolio to live the retirement he has envisioned.

I asked him what the value of his $2 million portfolio will be worth when he retires in two years. His response? "I have no idea." He was right! There is no way to know what your portfolio of stocks will be worth in two years. Maybe it will be worth $2.5 million; or maybe we'll have another market crash, and it will only be worth $1 million. It becomes a guessing game when you are trying to figure out where stocks are going to be in the short run.

This makes it impossible to plan. Because all his money is invested in stocks, he can't do any retirement planning.

Here's the clincher, though; he only needs $75,000 from his portfolio each year to live retirement the way he wants. That works out to be a yield of only 3.75 percent. If he were to shift his portfolio from stocks to income-producing investments as we discussed in the last chapter, then he could easily get $75,000 from interest and dividends without ever touching his principal. This would ensure a successful retirement no matter what the stock market does!

What if the market has a correction or crash before he retires and he never made that shift? What if the worst-case scenario happens, and his $2 million portfolio gets cut in half like it would have back in 2008 or 2001? Could he still get $75,000 per year? *No!* Because this would be a 7.5 percent withdrawal rate, which any financial advisor will tell you is completely unsustainable. He would be in grave danger of running out of money before running out of life no matter how he invested his portfolio. A substantial drop in the market could cost him his retirement! He is invested wrong for his stage of life, and if the market goes against him, his retirement may be on the line.

During the COVID crash of 2020, the market plummeted 37 percent in thirty-seven days,[15] the fastest drop in history.[16] As you know, it recovered by the end of 2020. This drop and recovery within a year was an anomaly, and many experts believe it was the unprecedented intervention of the massive stimulus packages that kept our economy from going into a depression. Will we be so lucky next time, though? No one knows.

Many experts believe, and market history seems to indicate, that we may have another crash looming on the horizon. And when that drop occurs, it could put a serious dent in your accumulated wealth right before you retire, wiping out much of what you have worked so hard to accumulate.

We all know people who planned to retire in 2009 but were not able to because of the market's downward turn in late 2007.

---

15   *Forbes*, "The Coronavirus Crash of 2020, and the Investing Lesson It Taught Us," February 11, 2021, https://www.forbes.com/sites/lizfrazierpeck/2021/02/11/the-coronavirus-crash-of-2020-and-the-investing-lesson-it-taught-us/?sh=58cb31dd46cf.

16   CNBC, "This Was the Fastest 30% Selloff Ever, Exceeding the Pace of Declines during the Great Depression," https://www.cnbc.com/2020/03/23/this-was-the-fastest-30percent-stock-market-decline-ever.html.

S&P 500 - 2007 TO 2021

TIME IT TOOK TO RETURN TO PREVIOUS HIGH

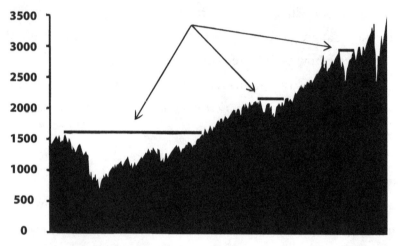

CHART E

On October 11, 2007, the S&P 500 Index hit a high of 1576. If you had $500,000 invested in the market on that day, you would have thought you were in pretty good shape. You would have thought that your plans to retire in 2009 looked safe, but you would have been wrong.

On March 9, 2009, only a year and a half later, the S&P 500 hit a low of 676, and you would have lost nearly 60 percent of your portfolio. That $500,000 that you had would have dwindled to $215,000. Yep—$285,000 of your retirement would have vanished into thin air. It might have taken you a decade to save that kind of dough only to have it wiped out in a year and a half.

The market wouldn't hit 1576 until April 10, 2013, but you would have still been a long way from getting back to even. Why? Because this does not account for fees or the loss of buying power you would have incurred due to inflation.

History is trying to warn us that we may be at this stage again in the near future. It's easy for people to think, "Well, I got five or seven years left. I'm okay because I'm still in the growth phase. I don't need to take withdrawals from my portfolio for a half a decade, so I've got nothing to worry about." Wrong. If you cannot afford to ride out another 50 percent crash in the market, then you shouldn't be taking the risk, especially if you are retired or within a decade of retirement. If you are nearing retirement age, and you are still invested for growth, you may be playing a risky game. If the market crashes, you may be forced to keep working through what were supposed to be your golden years, because a good chunk of your nest egg has vanished.

If you're already retired, it's even worse. Why? I will answer this question in the next chapter.

If you're in or nearing retirement and you're still fully invested in stocks, you have to ask yourself, in the infamous words of Clint Eastwood in the movie *Dirty Harry*, "Do you feel lucky?" Unfortunately, if the market drops by another 50 percent, it really doesn't matter whether you feel lucky or not. When the tide sinks, all the ships sink with it.

Let's Talk About Cash

A lot of people near or in retirement have already concluded that they cannot afford to take the risk of another market crash. Consequently, they have sold their stocks and put their money in the bank, where they don't have to worry about losing it. But this creates another risk: inflationary risk—that is, losing buying power to inflation. Most people don't realize how much buying power they will lose to inflation if they let their money sit idle in the bank.

Most people have never considered the effects of inflation on their retirement plan. This can be a grave mistake, especially since inflation has recently crept up more than it has in the last twenty years. Losing buying power is like a slow-growing cancer; you may not feel the effects right away, but if it's not treated, eventually it catches up to you—sometimes after it is too late.

It's been shown that the inflation rate for retirees is higher than the inflation rate for nonretirees. This is because retirees have time to spend money on things that they didn't really spend money on when they were working, like travel and other leisurely activities. And leisurely items tend to inflate more than the necessities.

There also may be a significant increase in healthcare expenditures. It's probably no secret that healthcare goes up faster than everything else, often inflating at a pace of 6 percent per year.[17] As we age, we are faced with more health concerns than we had when we were younger. In fact, many of us discover that we pay in our senior years for those activities we did when we were younger, when we thought we were invincible. The pounding we put on our feet from miles of running to stay fit, the muscle strains that we didn't properly take care of and allow to heal, the less than optimal dietary habits we got into when we were younger and may still adhere to. These things come back and give us a bill when we get older. Arthritis, joint replacement, high cholesterol, hardening of the arteries, cancer, and heart disease are all too real for too many seniors in America today.

Historically, the average inflation rates have been between 3 and 4 percent for the general populous. But retirees face real inflation rates between 4 and 5 percent. That's something you have to be prepared for. In an ironic twist of events, when you're retired and

17   The Balance, "The Rising Cause of Healthcare by Year and Its Causes," March 26, 2021, https://www.thebalance.com/causes-of-rising-healthcare-costs-4064878.

have less income, that is when you'll need more income. This is where many people make a huge mistake with their money. They put it in the bank. Simply because they don't know about the other alternatives that will provide them more interest without a lot of additional risk—certainly not the risk of a 50 percent loss that is inherent in the stock market.

Let's say you have half a million dollars, and you've got the money sitting in the bank earning 1 percent or less. If you have a half million dollars earning 1 percent, then you're getting $5,000 a year of interest. If it's not in a retirement account, you have to pay taxes on that. If your tax rate is 20 percent, then you have $4,000 left. That means your money is really earning only 0.8 percent after tax.

If inflation is 5 percent, then on a half a million dollars, you need to earn $25,000 a year in interest just to keep pace. What this literally means is that next year, you need to have $525,000

> *In an ironic twist of events, when you're retired and have less income, that is when you'll need more income.*

to buy the same goods and services that $500,000 buys you today. If you've only earned $4,000 because your money is sitting in the bank, then you're going backward by $21,000 every year. If you keep it there for a decade, you've lost $210,000 of buying power. If you keep your money in the bank for twenty years, you will have lost $420,000 worth of buying power. And if you're fortunate enough to live in retirement for thirty more years, then you will have lost over $630,000 of buying power over that time. That's a loss of more than your original investment in buying power! This is the effect that inflation could have on your purchasing power over a long period of time—which is why I refer to it as a slow-growing cancer.

Now imagine for a second that in today's mail, you receive a letter from your bank. This letter says, "We are so sorry, but our costs have increased dramatically, and we are forced to pass those costs onto the consumers. We need to begin charging you a fee of $1,750 a month for allowing you to keep your money on deposit with us—thank you for your business." Is there anything the bank could do to keep you from closing your accounts? Offer you chocolate cookies every time you come in? Call you every day? Of course, the answer is "nothing." The reality is that by losing $21,000 every year to inflation, that's the equivalent of writing a check for $1,750 to the bank every month! Don't get me wrong; it's not really the bank that is taking it from you, but economically speaking, the principle is the same. Every month you leave your cash in the bank, you're losing over $1,750 of buying power because of inflation. The banks are making money on your money; they're just not paying you for it.

What About Fixed Income?

We have already talked about the precarious position of the stock market and the "warm and fuzzy feeling" you should be getting from investing in stocks. Not.

Cash is certainly not a safe harbor either. Cash is generally paying 1 percent or less, and the historical inflation average is nearly triple that. As we discussed, if you store your assets in cash today, you are losing money.

What about fixed-income investments? When the phrase "fixed income" is mentioned, most investors think of bonds. Although bonds are one type of fixed income, there are many other types of investments that can be rightfully classified in this category. As the name suggests, your income is fixed, regardless of what the portfolio value is on any particular day. However, if you understand how bonds work, then you'll have a good handle on how the universe of other fixed-income investments work. Let's use bonds as a good illustration of fixed-income investing.

If you're looking for a safe, conservative investment, as boring as they are, individual bonds may be a good way to go. During a stock market crash, bonds become quite exciting, because you know your investments and your income are safe as long as you're invested in high-quality companies. But you have to be careful, because not all bonds are the same. And there is a significant difference between buying an individual bond and investing in a bond mutual fund. Often, when someone tells me they have bonds, they don't own individual bonds; they own bond mutual funds. If you invest in bonds through your retirement account, as is frequently the case, then you almost certainly have bond mutual funds.

You may have heard or read about bond bubbles and that people who have bonds are going to lose lots of money. The media has been big on touting that the bond bubble is going to burst. And if you don't know the difference between owning individual bonds or investing in bond mutual funds, you can get misled. Let's talk about the basic differences.

Individual Bonds

When you buy an individual bond, you are loaning the issuer money for a specified period of time and under predetermined terms. When you acquire an individual bond, you own the contract. As a result, you get the two guarantees that the contract offers.

The first guarantee is a set interest rate at which you shall accumulate interest payments. The second guarantee is that at some predetermined point down the road, called a "maturity date," you will get all your principal back, assuming that the bond issuer doesn't go bankrupt. As long as you hold the bond to maturity, you will get a guaranteed interest rate and you will get your principal back.

Between the time that you buy the bond and the time that the bond matures, the value of the bond itself is going to fluctuate. Regardless of the fluctuation, the interest payments to you will stay the same. If you hold it to maturity, you'll get your principal back. Therefore, the fluctuation does not affect you.

Let's look at a hypothetical example.

Let's say you invest $100,000 in a ten-year bond that is paying 4 percent. That bond is going to pay you $4,000 a year in interest. The value of your bond is going to fluctuate, but the $4,000 a year is going to stay the same.

There are a lot of reasons why bond values fluctuate, but one of the biggest factors has to do with interest rates. Bond values fluctuate opposite of interest rates. If interest rates go up, your bond value goes down and vice versa. Therefore, if you're investing in bonds, you should know where we are in the interest rate environment. Right now, interest rates are still historically low. As of the middle of 2021, the Fed Funds rate is at 0.25 percent. If you go back to 2000 and 2007, rates were hovering around 6 percent. If you go back to the eighties, rates were in double digits. Rates are at historic lows today compared to where they've been in history. And most professionals, including me, believe that interest rates are going to remain low for a long time. If rates do go up, though, the value of your bonds are going to drop on paper; but your interest payments are going to stay the same. When the bond matures, you're going to get your principal back.

If you are getting $4,000 per year of interest, and you get your $100,000 back when the bond matures, how much will any fluctuation along the way *really* affect you? Not at all. When you invest for income, as long as you're choosing companies that are solid, there is no concern about a bond bubble. The companies are going to have to go broke for you not to get paid.

Most investors today, however, are not invested in individual bonds. They're invested in bond funds. There are two reasons for this. The first reason is that most retirement plans only offer bond mutual funds, not individual bonds. The second reason is that advisors usually recommend bond mutual funds for their clients who want bonds. Why? Because bond funds are much easier to invest in than individual bonds, and brokers earn a residual commission only when they sell you a bond fund, not an individual bond.

There's a whole different skill set for selecting individual bonds as opposed to selecting a mutual fund. Anyone with a minimum amount of knowledge can select a mutual fund. All you have to do is check a box.

But here's the caveat: by investing in bond mutual funds, you no longer own the contract. You own the fund, which in turn owns the contracts. As a result, you lose the two most important guarantees that you get with individual bonds. Namely the guaranteed interest and the guarantee that you'll get your principal back. Bond mutual funds don't pay a specified interest rate, and the interest you receive is going to fluctuate. Furthermore, mutual funds never mature. If interest rates go up and the value of your individual bond goes down, that's just a paper loss, because as long as you hold it to maturity, you'll get your principal back. On the other hand, if interest rates go up and the value of your bond mutual fund goes down, that could be a permanent loss, because there is no maturity date. Therefore, with a bond fund, you lose the guarantee that you have with an individual bond.

Bond values have generally been going up for the last thirty years because interest rates have been steadily declining. This decline in rates over the last three decades has acted as a tailwind for bonds. Rates can't get much lower, and if they do turn around, that tailwind will turn into a headwind, causing the share price of bond funds to fall.

Interest rates aren't going to stay near zero forever. When they start to go back up, it will be at the expense of many bond fund investors who are unsuspecting and unaware. If they've got longer duration bonds, they're likely to drop even more when the interest rates start to go back up. This is because the longer term the bond, the more likely it is to react to changes in interest rates. There are bonds today that, if interest rates go back to where they were a decade ago, will possibly lose 20 or 25 percent of their value! This is why the media is touting a bond bubble.

Another problem of investing in bond funds is that you're subject to the panicky whims of other investors. Part of the problem is that people *think* that bond funds are safe. They don't know that a bond fund can actually lose value. When the share price of a bond fund starts dropping, it may scare a lot of people, causing them to panic and sell their shares, which may cause the bond fund to spiral down even further. You better hang on, because you can't control what the other investors do.

When you own the contract, *you* get to determine if and when to sell that bond. If rates suddenly go up another percent or more, causing the fund to drop 5 or 10 percent in value, many of these people may start thinking their investment doesn't seem as safe as they thought it was, and they may decide to bail out. When you own the contract, you are in control. You have the option of holding it to maturity so you can recover your principal.

If you own the contract, you're going to be all right. Unless you need to sell your bonds early, there is no bond bubble for you. The difference between owning individual bonds or investing in bond funds is the difference between doing the driving or being driven.

So, What's The Answer?

I believe that the better option is to invest in individual bonds, not bond funds, and to diversify. In effect, build your own bond fund. It is not a mutual fund, because it is only for you. It's a custom bond fund. You are the driver. Limit your investment in any one bond to a small percentage of your total bond investment: no more than 2 or 3 percent. Spread your investment across different types of bonds with the primary focus being on quality. Different types of bonds have different types of risk and give you different yields. Utility bonds are different from municipal bonds. Municipals are different from industrial bonds. Corporate bonds are different from both. If you take the time to understand what each bond represents, and what the maturity date, interest rate, and call provisions are, then you can stagger your maturity dates and principal reinvestment strategies so that you always have a steady stream of interest income from your investment. If you don't know how to do this, then you need to have an advisor who does. An advisor who specializes in income will be able to help you buy individual bonds for some portion of your portfolio and maximize your investment for the highest income.

Let's say you're considering buying corporate bonds. Where do you begin in your analysis? I would suggest that you begin with the credit rating. Corporations have credit ratings like we do. That's a good place to start because there are companies that have great credit, and there are companies that have bad credit. When companies with bad credit issue bonds, they are called *junk bonds*.

Just because a company has bad credit doesn't mean they're going broke. It's the same as our personal credit system, where we could end up with a poor credit rating after we get hit with medical bills after an unexpected surgery. When we want to take out a loan, our credit report is run the same way a corporation's is, and a credit rating is based on the FICO system. FICO is an acronym for the Fair Isaac Corporation, a data analytics company that was founded in 1956 by engineer William Fair and mathematician Earl Isaac.[18] Their credit scoring system is based on credit reports with scores ranging from 300 to 850.

Lenders use the scores to gauge a potential borrower's credit worthiness. If you're at 850, you have excellent credit and probably get truckloads of junk mail for 0 percent interest credit cards. If you have a credit score of 300, no lender wants to talk to you.

Somewhere in the midst of all that, the lender has to draw a demarcation line in the sand. Different lenders draw that line in different places depending on what their goals are. If you're above that line, then you're in great shape: you've got good credit. If you're below the line, you've got bad credit. For example, a lender may draw that line at 700. If you're at a 700 FICO score, you're good. If I'm at a 699 FICO score, I'm bad. You're prime; I'm subprime. You get the credit card with a preferred rate; I don't. But if you're at 700, and I'm at 699, does it really sound like there's a significant difference in risk? There's not, but they must draw the line somewhere.

Only after you meet the creditor's minimum credit score will they look at the other requirements. They look at whether you own or rent. Do you have a steady source of income that can support adding the additional payment? Do you pay your bills on time? What is your

---

18   The Balance, "What Is a FICO Score?," September 16, 2020, https://www.thebalance.com/fico-score-960648.

debt-to-income ratio? All of these and more are the different things they want to know before approving you for a loan.

It's similar with corporations, albeit a little more complicated. They don't have just one credit rating score that they use. There are actually three different companies that provide credit ratings for corporations: Standard & Poor's, Moody's, and Fitch.

Once you establish your initial search criteria and have a grasp on the credit ratings, the process of selecting good, quality investments becomes a lot easier. By limiting your investment to only 2 percent or so per bond, you are giving yourself a range of fifty different entities to consider. Or maybe you want to take a small portion of your capital and commit to a longer-term investment that is going to give you a steady stream of higher income. On top of that base, layer some medium- and short-term investments with varying maturity dates, giving you an even distribution of investments across different sectors of the economy. This will provide a dampening effect against any unexpected shocks to the financial system and give you the control you need to reconfigure your portfolio if the need arises.

The next thing to look at is the fundamentals of the company. One of the advantages of working with a seasoned, professional advisor is that they are going to be able to look at the numbers and see the trends and aberrations, clues that something is not as it seems. If you do it on your own and you make a mistake, you may very well buy a bond with a company that is in trouble.

If it looks good, that's a good start, but you must always remember the prime disclaimer for every investment: "Past performance is no guarantee of future results."

This includes bonds and bond funds. History does not necessarily reflect the present or the future performance of any investment. All of the variables that played a part in the past performance of that investment over a specific period of time are different. The economy is different. The market is different. The weather is different. The staff at the company has changed. Thousands and thousands of variables that all came together to cause a company to reach earnings high over the past fiscal year are all different. And you can never get them back in the exact same sequence of events or timing. It is a fool's errand to even try.

History does not necessarily reflect the present or the future performance of any investment.

The best course of action is to educate yourself and find an experienced advisor who can help you put together your proprietary portfolio with just the right mix of short-, medium-, and long-term investments that are going to be strong, dependable income generators for the long term. Get in the habit of periodically revisiting and tweaking your investment strategy as necessary.

I've only discussed bonds as one example of how fixed-income investing works. There are many other bond-like alternatives that work similarly. Without taking on a lot of additional risk, by creating a portfolio of fixed-income investments, you can collect your income each month without ever touching your principal.

CHAPTER FIVE

What You Don't Know about Investing for Growth Versus Income

WHEN I MEET with someone initially, the first thing I try to discover is the purpose for their money and what phase of life they're in. I want to get to know who they are, what they have accomplished in life, and their level of financial understanding and experience. I want to understand what their expectations are for their life going forward. What do they want their money to do for them? What is the plan for their money? Most people have never given this the attention it deserves. Most of the time I get some vague, ambiguous answer like, "I just want it to grow. I want it to last."

That's nice, but that doesn't tell me anything useful. I get excited when I sit down with someone and they start telling me about their lifelong desire to travel to Italy to visit the town from where their family immigrated, or their dream to go to China and walk on the Great Wall. I love when they tell me they want to have a condo in

Florida on the golf course or overlooking the beach and know that their bills are paid. It encourages me when they talk about being independent in their senior years and financially prepared for any unexpected medical expenses or long-term care.

So ... let me ask you, What is the goal of your money? What is its purpose? If you can't answer that question, then how do you know if your current investment strategy is supporting or conflicting it? If you don't have a target, how do you know if you've hit it? Or if you've missed it? You must know what the purpose of your money is and have a target so you can focus your energy on making sure that your investment and retirement strategies are supporting your purpose.

When you boil it down to its simplicity, there are generally only three possible purposes, or goals, for your money.

The first goal is that you're saving your money for a lump-sum purchase. This would be things like purchasing a home or a second home. It could be saving money to start your own business. You might be saving for a month-long tour of Europe or a cruise around the South Pacific. You might be thinking about buying a parcel of land that you've always wanted to develop or a rental property that you can rehab to have a residual income. You might be saving money to pay for your daughter's wedding or your grandchildren's college. You might want to pay off your child's student loans when they graduate from college. These are all legitimate goals for your money. If you hope to use a portion of your money to make a future lump-sum purchase, identifying this will help you invest this money now so that it supports that purpose later.

The second goal for your money may be to leave it as a legacy. You might want to leave an endowment at your alma mater, your church, or another favorite charity.

Some people are sacrificing in this life and saving as much as they can so they can leave as much as possible to their children. Maybe they have a special-needs child, or they think that life is going to be harder in the future. They're willing to make that sacrifice. They are intentionally spending less now so their children can have more in the future. This is a legitimate purpose for your money.

For most people, though, leaving a legacy is a secondary goal. They want whatever is left to go to their family after they are gone, but their primary purpose, the third common goal, is for their money to go toward retirement—to give them income after they stop working. If this is the purpose of your money, then you want to have the cash flow you need to support your lifestyle, adjust for inflation, and make sure you never run out of money in retirement regardless of how long you live. You are not just putting money away for savings' or investment's sake. You are purchasing your freedom on the installment plan. By far, this is the most common purpose for a retiree's money—to use it to provide income during retirement.

As we've been discussing, if you want to make sure your money is supporting your goal, then it's pretty important to know exactly what the purpose of your money will be, because the investment strategies will be different for each goal. The strategies employed to save for a lump-sum purchase down the road will be different from those that will be employed to save for retirement. And the strategies used to save for retirement are different than those that would be used when the purpose of your money is to leave a legacy. Therefore, you must know the purpose of your money so you can make sure your strategies are supporting your purpose. That's why I ask a lot of questions when I meet with people—so I can discover what the purpose of their money is.

If there is a problem, some component of their investment or retirement strategy that is conflicting with their purpose, my job is to discover it. I hasten to add, almost everyone I meet with has a problem of some sort that is causing them mental or emotional discomfort. There's an unknown that is lurking in the grayness beyond their perception. They can't physically see it or hear it, but they sense it is there, and it is causing them unease about the future. We don't know what we don't know. Feeling like there is a problem but not knowing what it is can create a retirement full of stress. I want you to have a stress-free retirement so you can sleep well.

> *Feeling like there is a problem but not knowing what it is can create a retirement full of stress. I want you to have a stress-free retirement so you can sleep well.*

Albert Einstein was asked about how he went about solving a problem. He replied that if he had an hour to solve a problem, he'd spend fifty-five minutes thinking about the problem and five minutes solving it.[19] Likewise, Abraham Lincoln said, "Give me six hours to chop down a tree, I will spend the first four sharpening the axe."[20] Translation: it takes time and effort to prepare for retirement. As a result, most retirees I meet have not properly prepared. They're not equipped for twenty or thirty years of life after they retire, and what makes this worse is that they don't even realize it. Until you identify the problem, you will never find a solution.

The very act of going through the process of identifying the problem reduces anxiety and may even eliminate the fear of the issue.

---

19 Quote Investigator, "I Would Spend 55 Minutes Defining the Problem and then 5 Minutes Solving It," https://quoteinvestigator.com/2014/05/22/solve/.

20 RainmakerVT, "Give Me Six Hours to Chop Down a Tree, and I Will Spend the First Four Sharpening the Axe," http://go.rainmakervt.com/resultsmailvt/2017/1/10/give-me-six-hours-to-chop-down-a-tree-and-i-will-spend-the-first-four-sharpening-the-axe.

Most problems usually arise when someone learns that their current investment strategies conflict with their goals.

One of the most common and concerning problems most retirees don't know about is that they aren't invested properly for the phase of life that they're in. Your life has two very distinct and separate phases. There is the growth phase, or accumulation phase, of life, where the goal is to accumulate and grow your money. Then there is the phase where you begin to take distributions from the funds that you have accumulated. I refer to this as the income phase, or distribution phase, of life. The accumulation phase is when you're putting money into your retirement accounts and saving for retirement, and the distribution phase is when you're withdrawing money from your retirement accounts. The investment strategies for each phase are completely different, yet most retirees are oblivious to this. They continue investing in retirement using the same strategies as when they were heading toward retirement.

The Accumulation Phase

During the accumulation phase, your goal should be to grow your nest egg as big as you can. That's your money's purpose. Why? Because when you get to retirement, you'll want to start living off what you have accumulated. Your focus during the first two-thirds of your projected life span should be on growth.

The most popular way to grow your assets is through dollar cost averaging. Dollar cost averaging is when you periodically buy the same dollar amount of investments over and over again, regardless of the price. This strategy drives the average purchase price of the investment down, which is what you want, right? If you're putting money into a retirement plan every paycheck, you are dollar cost averaging. Many people who have never heard of the term or don't know what it means are using this strategy to their advantage.

Here is an example of how this works. Let's say you are investing $100 per paycheck into a mutual fund. This paycheck, the mutual fund is priced at $10 per share. Therefore, if you invest $100 into it, you would have received 10 shares of that mutual fund, right? But let's say that during the next paycheck, the mutual fund drops to $5 per share. Because you're dollar cost averaging, you still invest $100. But this time, how many shares did you get? The answer is 20. Here's the final question: What is your average price per share? If you answered $7.50, you would be among the majority. This seems logical, because you paid $10 per share the first time and $5 per share the second time. Therefore, most people conclude that the average price per share is split down the middle at $7.50.

What they fail to consider, though, is that they received twice as many shares the second round as they did the first. The first round they bought 10 shares for $100, and the second round they bought 20 shares for $100, because the share price was cut in half. Therefore, they have bought a total of 30 shares for $200. This comes out to an average purchase price of $6.67 per share, not $7.50. By investing the same dollar amount into the same mutual fund repeatedly, you drive the average purchase price down, which is what you want to do. That is why dollar cost averaging is a popular and highly touted way to save for retirement when you're in the growth phase of life.

Once you reach the distribution phase of life, this strategy doesn't work so well. When you are invested for growth the only way to get the cash you need from your portfolio each month is to sell shares. Yep, that's it. It's often referred to as reverse dollar cost averaging. Dollar cost averaging is good. Reverse dollar cost averaging is not. Why? By selling shares, you drive the average sale price down, which is just the opposite of what you want to do. Every month you sell shares, you will have fewer shares to sell the next month, and the following month, and so on. You're eating into your principal every month that you make a withdrawal from your portfolio. Because paying your bills is not optional, even in retirement, every time the stock market goes down, it forces you to sell more shares to get the same income, because the price of each share is less. The downward decline in the stock market results in an even faster cannibalization of your principal. If you continue in this downward spiral and live long enough, what is likely to happen? You may run out of money before your final birthday. That's why being invested for growth when you are taking income from your portfolio can be so detrimental to your retirement.

Often, though, someone will tell me that they're not worried about dipping into their principal because they are only taking a small amount each month. I frequently hear that they are "only withdrawing 4 percent each year," following the 4 percent rule, which is a decades-old rule that gives you a general guideline for safely withdrawing from your portfolio. As the name indicates, if you're invested for growth, you can theoretically withdraw 4 percent per year from your portfolio and never have to worry about running out of money.

That's the general principle that's been touted; however, over the last few years, this rule has been challenged. Originally gaining traction in the eighties when interest rates were double digits, experts are questioning whether the 4 percent rule is still applicable now that interest rates have been in the single digits for the last twenty years.

In 2013, Morningstar did an analysis of this rule, and after analyzing it ten ways to Sunday, they concluded that the 4 percent rule was no longer applicable. The new rule, according to their studies, is the 2.8 percent rule.[21] Therefore, if you're invested for growth, you can only withdraw 2.8 percent per year without having to worry about running out of money. Based on this updated rule, someone with a $1 million portfolio can only withdraw $28,000 each year, not $40,000, if they don't want to worry about running out of money before they die.

Most people have never done the math. They errantly believe that it won't hurt them to just take a little bit of principal each year to provide them with the additional income they need. If they live long enough, however, there is a chance that their portfolio balance will expire before they do.

Think about how a fixed-rate, thirty-year mortgage works. When you make your first payment, is that payment all principal or all interest? Interest. I remember making my first mortgage payment many eons ago: I think I paid something like five dollars in principal! "How am I ever going to pay this thing off?" I thought. But by continuing to make monthly payments over time, the amount of principal being paid goes up, and the amount of interest being paid goes down. And after thirty years, the mortgage magically disappears—for one reason: because you consistently paid a little bit of principal every month over a long period of time.

Well, if the concept of paying a little bit of principal each month toward your mortgage causes it to disappear in thirty years, wouldn't the same concept hold true with your retirement withdrawals? Wouldn't it be true that, if all you did was consistently withdraw a little bit of principal from your retirement accounts each month, after thirty years your principal would have disappeared? The concept is exactly the same.

---

21   Morningstar, "Low Bond Yields and Safe Portfolio Withdrawal Rates," January 21, 2013, http://news.morningstar.com/pdfs/blanchett_lowbondyield_1301291.pdf.

I want to drive the point home by showing you a chart you'll find extremely eye opening.

INVESTMENT 1				
Date	Initial Cash	S&P 500	Income	End Cash
01/2000	$1,000,000	-9.10%	40,000.00	$861,306
01/2001	$861,306	-11.89%	40,000.00	$712,918
01/2002	$712,918	-22.10%	40,000.00	$510,267
01/2003	$510,267	28.68%	40,000.00	$598,627
01/2004	$598,627	10.88%	40,000.00	$609,722
01/2005	$609,722	4.91%	40,000.00	$586,785
01/2006	$586,785	15.79%	40,000.00	$623,763
01/2007	$623,763	5.49%	40,000.00	$606,173
01/2008	$606,173	-37.13%	40,000.00	$342,282
01/2009	$342,282	26.46%	40,000.00	$374,757
01/2010	$374,757	15.06%	40,000.00	$378,070
01/2011	$378,070	2.11%	40,000.00	$338,591
01/2012	$338,591	16.05%	40,000.00	$342,787
01/2013	$342,787	32.39%	40,000.00	$399,358
01/2014	$399,358	13.69%	40,000.00	$402,387
01/2015	$402,387	1.38%	40,000.00	$359,614
01/2016	$359,614	11.96%	40,000.00	$351,343
01/2017	$351,343	21.83%	40,000.00	$376,070
01/2018	$376,070	-4.38%	40,000.00	$315,944
01/2019	$315,944	31.49%	40,000.00	$363,021
01/2020	$363,021	18.40%	40,000.00	$374,897
01/2021	$374,897	28.71%	40,000.00	$430,877

TABLE C

This chart illustrates what the balance of a $1 million portfolio would have turned into if the 4 percent rule was used to withdraw funds based on the actual performance of the S&P 500 between 2000 and 2021. In other words, if someone had $1 million invested for growth in the stock market between 2000 and 2021, and they sold shares to withdraw $3,333 per month—$40,000 per year or 4 percent)—what would their balance be in 2021 based on actual stock market performance? Take a minute to study the table on the previous page.

You'll notice that the balance has dropped nearly 60 percent down to $430,877—all for the purpose of selling shares each month to withdraw 4 percent. So, you tell me: Does the 4 percent rule work? If you retired at sixty-five years old, you would be only eighty-five by the time 60 percent of your portfolio had vanished. How are you feeling with only 40 percent of your original principal intact, knowing that the remaining balance may need to last you another fifteen years or more? And you haven't even adjusted for inflation!

The period from 2000 to 2021 was not an anomaly for the stock market. There were only five negative years during this period. And the market was only negative once during the final decade. Yet despite this, the $1 million portfolio lost almost 60 percent of its value because shares were being sold to withdraw 4 percent per year.

Reverse dollar cost averaging to get your income can devastate your retirement. Most people underestimate the negative result of selling shares to pay their bills each month. I'm convinced that there is a wave of baby boomers who are in danger of running out of money when they get into their eighties. Now that you know this, you can protect yourself so you are not one of them.

The Distribution Phase

What's the alternative? You can invest for income in lieu of investing for growth. Let's suppose that instead of having to sell shares to get your income, you were getting 4 percent interest on your $1 million, regardless of how stocks did. The end result is displayed on the next page. Take a look at the "End Cash" column. How much of your investment is remaining after each withdrawal?

All of it. Because you did not sell shares to get your income each month.

Your interest has become a renewable resource. If you have $1 million invested in a bond, for example, that pays you 4 percent per year, that's $40,000 per year of interest. If you spend that $40,000 this year, how much interest can you expect to receive again next year? $40,000. And you can spend it again and again, year after year, because it never runs out, since you're not selling shares to get it. Therefore, by investing for income, you have protected your principal and have still been able to receive the income you either need or want.

		INVESTMENT 2		
Date	Initial Cash	S&P 500	Income	End Cash
01/2000	$1,000,000	4.00%	40,000.00	$1,000,000
01/2001	$1,000,000	4.00%	40,000.00	$1,000,000
01/2002	$1,000,000	4.00%	40,000.00	$1,000,000
01/2003	$1,000,000	4.00%	40,000.00	$1,000,000
01/2004	$1,000,000	4.00%	40,000.00	$1,000,000
01/2005	$1,000,000	4.00%	40,000.00	$1,000,000
01/2006	$1,000,000	4.00%	40,000.00	$1,000,000
01/2007	$1,000,000	4.00%	40,000.00	$1,000,000
01/2008	$1,000,000	4.00%	40,000.00	$1,000,000
01/2009	$1,000,000	4.00%	40,000.00	$1,000,000
01/2010	$1,000,000	4.00%	40,000.00	$1,000,000
01/2011	$1,000,000	4.00%	40,000.00	$1,000,000
01/2012	$1,000,000	4.00%	40,000.00	$1,000,000
01/2013	$1,000,000	4.00%	40,000.00	$1,000,000
01/2014	$1,000,000	4.00%	40,000.00	$1,000,000
01/2015	$1,000,000	4.00%	40,000.00	$1,000,000
01/2016	$1,000,000	4.00%	40,000.00	$1,000,000
01/2017	$1,000,000	4.00%	40,000.00	$1,000,000
01/2018	$1,000,000	4.00%	40,000.00	$1,000,000
01/2019	$1,000,000	4.00%	40,000.00	$1,000,000
01/2020	$1,000,000	4.00%	40,000.00	$1,000,000
01/2021	$1,000,000	4.00%	40,000.00	$1,000,000
01/2022	$1,000,000	4.00%	40,000.00	$1,000,000

TABLE D

"But don't I have to take more risk if I want to get more income?"
I often get asked. Ironically, the answer is no. Generally, investments

that focus on income have less risk than investments that are growth oriented. Whenever you tie an income to a portfolio, it narrows the fluctuation. The price can't get too low. It can't get too high. It is still going to fluctuate, and it is almost always much less volatile. But let's say, for the sake of argument, that your income portfolio did fluctuate as much as the market. Your million dollars would have dropped to roughly $500,000 in 2001 and bounced back to a million in 2006. Then starting in 2007, the downward spiral started again, and your million would have been turned into roughly $400,000 before hitting bottom. It would have taken roughly five years for your million to claw its way back to its original value.

Take a look at the following chart that shows the performance of the S&P 500 from 2000 to 2013. How much growth has there been? None, zero, zilch, nada. There have been two crashes and two recoveries but no growth. If you were selling shares to get your income every month, what would have happened to your portfolio balance over this time?

What if you were invested for income? What if you were simply living off the interest? Thirteen years later, your million dollars would still be the same as it was when you started withdrawing income. The difference is that this time, your portfolio was wisely invested for income. You would have been receiving that $40,000 every year from dividends and interest without ever having to sell a single share. How much did all that market volatility affect you?

Not at all. Because interest is a renewable resource; it will be there again next year regardless of portfolio value.

That's the difference between investing for growth and investing for income. Investing for growth requires you to sell shares to pay your bills. Investing for income allows you to keep your shares intact and still get your income. Here's a rhetorical question for you: Would you rather sell shares of your portfolio to get the cash you need every month to pay the bills, or would you rather not sell shares and still get the cash? You can ride out market volatility through the peaks and troughs if you are in the accumulation phase; but if you're in the income phase, you cannot ride this out.

GSPC YAHOO FINANCE CHART

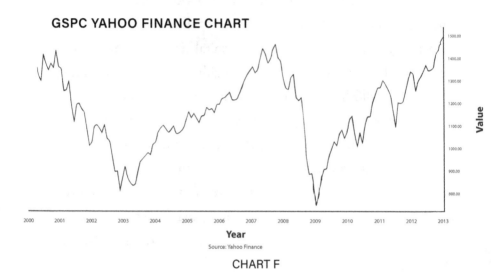

Source: Yahoo Finance

CHART F

You may not have enough time or resources to recover your losses. My fear for people who want to retire in the next five to ten years is that they are gambling with their future, and they might get caught in the downward part of the cycle, which I often refer to as the trough. I don't want them to get caught in the trough. We all know people who planned to retire in 2001 and 2008 but couldn't because they got caught in the trough.

As we've already discussed in the last chapter, the stock market went through two crashes and two recoveries between 2000 and 2013, resulting in a zero return. Your stock-based mutual funds would have followed suit, providing no growth over that time. If you started off in 2000 with a $1 million portfolio, it would have gone through a roller coaster ride and still have been worth $1 million thirteen years later (not taking into account fees and loss of buying power to inflation) if you were not withdrawing from it.

What if you were invested for income during this same period? You would have received your interest every year regardless of market performance. If you're receiving $40,000 of interest on your $1 million portfolio, and the market drops that year, you still get your $40,000. Year after year, you keep getting your $40,000 of interest. You would have started with $1 million and ended with $1 million. But this time, you would have collected $40,000 per year of income every year regardless of market performance. You would have received well over $500,000 of income. If you chose to reinvest the interest and dividends instead of spending them, your portfolio would have grown to over $1.5 million during the time that the market produced zero return! Not too shabby.

Because this is different than most people think, I want to give you one more powerful example. Imagine for a second that your retirement portfolio consists of a thirty-unit condominium complex. This is your retirement and needs to last the rest of your life. You have two options as to how you want to get the income you need from it each year. Option one is that you can sell one condo each year and live off the proceeds for that year. With this option, next year you'll only have twenty-nine units left, and the following year you'll only have twenty-eight units left and so on. Option two, however, is that you can rent out the entire complex and live off the rent without ever selling off any units. Which option do you choose? The first option, where you are reducing the number of condos you have each year? Or the second option, where you are protecting your condos but still receiving the same income? The answer is obvious.

If you are invested in the stock market and make withdrawals from your portfolio, you have selected option one for your portfolio, selling units to get your income. You probably did not realize that this is what you were doing. When you are invested for income, however, you are collecting "rent" from your portfolio while protecting your units. We just call this "rent" interest and dividends.

I can hear some of you asking, "Anthony, that's all nice and good, but can I really get 4 percent in today's low interest rate environment? Is that realistic?" Absolutely! You should be able to do better than that. Because most advisors specialize in growth-related investments, however, they're ill-equipped to help you. Because my firm specializes in income-producing strategies, our goal is to get our clients 4 to 5 percent of income per year after fees. If you only need to withdraw 4 percent per year from your portfolio, but you are receiving 5 percent of interest and dividends each year, your portfolio should actually grow despite your withdrawals. When you begin to realize that this is how investing for income works, you'll start to get excited. The reason they call it "fixed income" is because your income is fixed.

When you get near or are already in retirement, your focus should no longer be on the higher risk of growth. Your focus should change to the less risky strategies of preservation and income. As mentioned previously, there are two phases in life, accumulation and income. The strategies for helping you grow your money are completely different from the strategies that help you preserve your money. If you're in the growth phase of life, dollar cost averaging works very well. When your life makes a paradigm shift from the accumulation phase to the distribution phase, and you begin to reverse dollar cost average, it could be one of the most dangerous things you can do financially. If you're selling shares to get the cash you need out of your portfolio, the odds are that, if you live a long life as you hope, you may run out of money before you run out of life. Investing for income will dramatically increase your odds of solving this problem. Now you know.

CHAPTER SIX

What You Don't Know about Long-Term Care

If you fail to plan, you are planning to fail.

—BENJAMIN FRANKLIN

I OFTEN THINK I should have this Ben Franklin quote displayed over the entryway to my office. It is the gospel for financial planners and advisors because it applies to everyone. We don't know how long you're going to live and what your health will look like when you retire, or if you'll be able to afford your present lifestyle several years from now. The only thing we know for sure is that we are all going to get older and eventually die.

There is an urban legend about seniors who are healthy when they reach their later years. They don't feel confident that they can live on their own any longer, but they don't want to live in a nursing home. So they are booking nonstop, back-to-back passages on cruise ships because it is cheaper than a nursing home. The food is better, and you can stay as active as you want or just sit on the deck and read a book in the fresh ocean air.

"What happens when you run out of money?" I asked the man who told me about this.

"Well," he said with a chuckle, "I was told there was always the option of going for a midnight stroll off the fantail."

That doesn't sound like a serious plan to me. It may sound like a romantic way to go, but how many sane, rational people will jump off the back end of a ship twenty stories above the ocean in the middle of the night just because they are running out of money? Besides, I'm pretty sure the insurance companies would enact a rule prohibiting three consecutive cruises if this kind of "exit strategy" ever became a trend.

My friend Greg Melia, a financial advisor in Tulsa, Oklahoma, came up with a way to look at the retirement years of the baby boomers. Greg divides the retirement years into three different age periods.

The first period starts at retirement and usually continues through the seventies. This is the period we call the "go-go" years. These are the golden years of your life and the reason you have worked and saved for the last thirty to forty years in your job or your profession. This is the time when you can finally do the things you want to do and go where you want to go. Maybe it's taking a cruise or volunteering your time and talents to work for the benefit of others. Maybe it is pursuing a new hobby or taking a class in a subject that interests you. At this stage, life is a symphony, and you are the conductor.

The honeymoon period of the "go-go" years lasts for a decade or more in many cases. But somewhere in the late seventies or early eighties, retired people tend to slow down.

We call this phase of retirement the "slow-go" years. For most retirees, this is going to consume a decade or so of their retirement—often starting in the late seventies and continuing to the late eighties.

During this time, you become more reflective about life and your role in it. You look back on your own journey and try to find the markers that indicate a life well lived. You savor the time that you get to spend with your children and your grandchildren, because you know that they are your only true legacy. You look for ways to make your time count every day. Sometimes there may be health issues that cause a person to slow down and take it easy, but most of the time it is just a matter of choosing to slow down and notice the wonder of life in the moment and being present. Self-awareness, reflection, and deep appreciation are acquired life skills that often take a lifetime to master.

Sir Isaac Newton stated in his second law of motion that the rate of change in a body's momentum is equal to the net force acting on it.[22] As you enter your nineties, the wear and tear of living life begins to manifest on and in your body in a big way. There are certainly exceptions; but for most people, everything seems to take more effort than it did the last time you tried it. You don't walk as fast. You don't jump as high. In fact, you don't jump at all for fear of falling and not being able to get up. We often refer to this period of life as the "no-go" years. Even if you could go somewhere, you generally don't want to. This is a time when you would rather read a book, watch television, or do a crossword puzzle to keep your brain active.

For most of us, it is this "no-go" phase of our lives where we are going to need long-term care. The problem is that if we wait until we need it to purchase it, we probably won't qualify and won't be able to afford it anyway. But what exactly is long-term care? Let's explore

---

22   Wikipedia, "Newton's Laws of Motion," accessed April 21, 2022, https://en.wikipedia.org/wiki/Newton's_laws_of_motion.

what the Department of Health and Human Services (HHS) says about this.

Long-term care is a range of services and support you may need to meet your personal care needs. Most long-term care is not medical care but rather assistance with the basic personal tasks of everyday life, referred to as activities of daily living (ADLs), such as the following:

- Transferring (from bed or chair)

- Dressing

- Using the toilet

- Bathing

- Eating

- Caring for incontinence

Other common long-term care services and supports are assistance with everyday tasks, sometimes called instrumental activities of daily living (IADLs), including the following:

- Housework

- Taking medication

- Shopping for groceries

- Caring for pets

- Managing money

- Preparing and cleaning up after meals

- Using the telephone or other communication devices

- Responding to emergency alerts such as fire alarms

If you are sixty-five years old, HHS data suggests that there is a 52 percent chance that there is going to come a period of your life when you are not going to be able to get out of bed, wash your face, and brush your teeth. If you need this kind of help, you are either going to pay for it out of your own pocket or, if you planned ahead and purchased long-term care insurance, the insurance company will pay for these services for you. Unless you have a stroke or some other medical condition that comes on suddenly, it is not likely that you are going to wake up healthy and vital one morning and then wake up the next day and require all those services. Long-term care dependency usually occurs over a period. The instrumental activities of daily living become more challenging. Then the basic ADLs start becoming issues. Slowly but surely, you go from a fairly independent person who needs someone to do light housekeeping to a "shut-in" requiring around-the-clock monitoring and attention. These may be things that your family can help you with, but what if you are living in Florida and your family is living in the suburbs of Chicago?

LONG-TERM CARE COSTS TODAY		
National Average		Monthly
Skilled Nursing Facility	Private Room	$9,360
	Semiprivate Room	$8,190
Assisted Living Facility	One Bedroom/Month	$4,797
Registered Nurse	One Home Visit/Day	$4,410
In-Home Healthcare	24-Hour Aide On-Site	$18,720

Source: Lincoln Financial Group, "What Care Costs," December 25, 2021, https://www.whatcarecosts.com/Sponsor#/.

TABLE E

Now ask yourself, "Do I really want to depend on my children for this?"

According to Longtermcare.gov, about 70 percent of people turning age sixty-five can expect to use some form of long-term care during their lives.[23]

What are some of the average national costs associated with long-term care? The Long Term Care Group (LTCG) of Eden Prairie, Minnesota,[24] is the nation's premier provider of long-term care administration services and the subject-matter experts in the cost of long-term care. LTCG annually surveys more than thirty thousand LTC service providers across the nation to collect cost-of-care data. That data is analyzed and quantified at the national, state, and metropolitan statistical area level to obtain an average of all costs. I have chosen a few to give you a snapshot view of some of the average national costs associated with housing in a skilled nursing facility or an assisted living facility. I have also included the costs of having an RN visit your home daily and the costs of having a licensed home healthcare aide in your home on a twenty-four-hour basis.

According to Longtermcare.gov, about 70 percent of people turning age sixty-five can expect to use some form of long-term care during their lives.

These costs vary from state to state. Alaska is the most expensive, followed by Connecticut. I live in California, which is ranked nineteenth. The least expensive state is Oklahoma. As you can see, the act

23   LongTermCare.gov, "How Much Care Will You Need?," https://acl.gov/ltc/basic-needs/how-much-care-will-you-need#:~:text=Someone%20turning%20age%2065%20today,for%20longer%20than%205%20years.

24   LTCG, "Cost of Care," https://www.ltcg.com/our-services/cost-of-care/.

of growing older and requiring assistance due to failing health is a costly proposition, and it's not going to get any cheaper.

LTCG has projected how these costs will continue to rise. For the purposes of providing a snapshot of their extensive data, I have chosen projections for our three sample states for ten years from today and twenty years from today.

Unfortunately, we live in a time when our social norms seem to be determined by the television programs we watched growing up. When it comes to end-of-life planning, we seem to have an epidemic known as Walton's Syndrome, where we imagine we are fully aware and surrounded by our loved ones when we take our last breath.

SAMPLE OF LONG-TERM CARE COSTS BY STATE/PROJECTION OVER 20 YEARS			
Connecticut	**Monthly Today**	**2029***	**2039***
Skilled Nursing Facility			
Private Room	$13,916	$16,964	$20,678
Semiprivate Room	$12,669	$15,480	$18,870
Assisted Living Facility			
One-Bedroom	$4,880	$5,949	$7,251
Registered Nurse			
One Home Visit/Day	$2,625		
In-Home Healthcare			
24-Hour Health Aide Onsite	$17,280	$21,067	$25,675
California	**Monthly Today**	**2029***	**2039***
Skilled Nursing Facility			
Private Room	$10,646	$12,977	$15,819
Semiprivate Room	$8,760	$10,678	$13,017
Assisted Living Facility			
One-Bedroom	$4,500	$5,485	$6,687
Registered Nurse			
One Home Visit/Day	$2,625		
In-Home Healthcare			
24-Hour Health Aide Onsite	$20,160	$24,573	$29,959
Oklahoma	**Monthly Today**	**2029***	**2039***
Skilled Nursing Facility			
Private Room	$5,627	$6,859	$8,361
Semiprivate Room	$4,867	$5,933	$7,232
Assisted Living Facility			
One-Bedroom	$3,518	$4,288	$5,228
Registered Nurse			
One Home Visit/Day	$2,625		
In-Home Healthcare			
24-Hour Health Aide Onsite	$16,020	$19,526	$23,803
*Projections for Long-Term Care costs are based on a 2 percent inflation rate			

TABLE F

That is about as realistic as entertaining the notion that your children will take you in and care for you in your later years. It sounds noble and altruistic, but it rarely ever resembles anything close to real life. Just a few months ago, I had a woman come in for a consultation, and while she liked many of the suggestions I had given her for restructuring her portfolio and moving some of her assets around, she disagreed with my suggestions for long-term care insurance.

"Oh, I don't need that," she said. "My daughter is very successful and makes a lot of money. She has a beautiful home with a guest suite that I stay in whenever I go for a visit. I'm pretty sure she will have me move in with her when the time comes."

"That sounds pretty good," I said. "But can you at least ask her about her plans before we go forward with your plan? Her input could affect how we proceed with what we have talked about." The lady promised me that she would have a chat with her daughter to make sure we were all on the same page.

I called a week later, but she had not been able to get in touch with her daughter due to business travel. The week after that, her daughter had some scheduling conflicts. The next two weeks, my call went to voice mail. She answered the following week and told me her daughter had been preoccupied with preparing to attend a conference in London and was then going for a two-week ski vacation in Switzerland with her husband.

"But I promise, Anthony, as soon as she gets back, she and I will have a conversation."

"May I point out the obvious?" I asked her. "You have not been able to have a ten-minute conversation in two months about your end-of-life plans with the person you believe is going to take care of you in the future. Can you understand why I might, as your financial advisor, have some serious concerns about a positive outcome here?"

There was silence on the other end of the phone, and I was pretty sure she was about to fire me.

"You're right," she sighed. "Who am I kidding? I raised her to be independent and live life to the fullest. It probably wouldn't even occur to her that I would be expecting her to give that up. I guess we better look at that long-term care policy."

That's the flip side to the end-of-life planning scenario. We raise our children to grow up, be independent, and live their own lives. We have taught them to be successful and enjoy the fruits of their labor. Then when we start to talk about a plan for long-term care, we think our kids are going to drop everything? Why? Because we think the premium is too high?

Sometimes it is because we are concerned about running out of money. If you have done your due diligence and worked out a comprehensive plan for retirement, this won't be an issue until you are well past one hundred years old. You may not be able to avoid finding yourself living in the outskirts of "no-go" land, but solid financial planning and then living within the parameters of that plan will ensure that you won't be there due to lack of funding.

I find that a lot of retirees find ways to live within their means. Some will balk at a discussion of long-term care, but the majority will realize the value of not burdening their family. They ask me what they can expect to get from their portfolio that will give them a comfortable lifestyle, and then they adjust their desires accordingly. Yes, it would be nice to have a condo on the golf course in a gated community in Florida or a hacienda on a cliff overlooking the Pacific Ocean in Cabo San Lucas, but is it financially responsible to do that knowing that you are leaving the long-term care responsibility to your spouse or children?

Life is not just about working. It is also about living and loving. Love is what makes a house a home and a group of relatives a family, and you have a responsibility to protect that legacy of love. You have the responsibility to not only protect your independence but also the independence of your children.

Sometimes the hard choices are forced upon us by mental health issues. We may suffer from dementia or Alzheimer's disease. We may be suffering from loneliness, a sense of our own mortality, or depression. As much as is humanly possible, we should fight sliding into this gray waiting room of life. This is time when the old adage "use it or lose it" should become our daily mantra. We may not be able to do a 5k walk, but we really do need to make the effort to keep our minds engaged and active.

I have clients who have told me that they have joined social clubs like the Red Hat Society or Toastmasters so they can be around people with similar interests who will keep them engaged and interested. Others volunteer at their church and spend their time helping others. It keeps them alert and present to be there for somebody else.

Everybody believes they are going to be aware of what is going on around them right up to the end of their life. Unfortunately, that is simply not the reality today. There are more and more people these days that physically arrive at the tail end of their golden years, but they are not there to enjoy them with their friends and family. They are mentally gone. In too many cases, this occurs long before they physically die.

Nobody expects to spend their last years on Earth shuffling slowly toward the Fields of Forgotten. All the wonderful life memories morph into abandoned sandcastles that were built on the beach in low tide and fade away with the pull of the waves. Instead of a legacy of cherished memories, too many are left with an inheritance of resentment.

According to AARP, only 7.2 million or so Americans have long-term care insurance.[25] That's less than 3 percent of adult Americans. Most make the inaccurate assumption that they're never going to need it or it's too expensive. The sooner you plan for long-term care, the better.

Won't Medicare cover long-term care? I get asked this all the time. Generally, Medicare does not cover custodial care if that is the only type of care that is needed. Medicare will offer coverage only if two basic requirements are met:

- The care is considered medically necessary and prescribed by a licensed physician or authorized medical personnel.

- The care is conducted by a healthcare provider who participates in Medicare.

The kicker is that even if a patient meets both of these requirements, Medicare will only cover a hundred days of nursing care. The rest is on you.

On the other hand, Medicaid is a needs-based social program that covers custodial care if it is provided within a nursing facility. The requirements and services for coverage vary widely from state to state. I live in California. The California version of Medicaid is called Medi-Cal. Both Medi-Cal and Medicaid provide a core set of health benefits, including doctor visits, hospital care, immunization, pregnancy-related services, and nursing home care. It also covers mental health and substance use disorder services, including behavioral health treatment. Prescription drugs are also covered.

To be eligible for Medicaid, beneficiaries would have to first pay for basic custodial care out-of-pocket. Only when their assets have been used up will Medicaid kick in. Custodial care at home is typically covered only by long-term care insurance—not by Medicaid. Medicaid covers custodial care while it is provided in a nursing facility.

This spend-down requirement is becoming a horror story for many Americans. A friend of mine recently shared the story of her mother, Gloria. Gloria had exercised her whole life, had eaten healthy, did all the right things, didn't drink, and didn't smoke. After her husband died, Gloria never remarried. Instead, she finished her career as a bank manager and retired. She chose to live a full social life, did some traveling, and spent a lot of time doting on her grandchildren. At age seventy, she and her thirteen-year-old grandson white water rafted down the Green River.

Five years later, she was diagnosed with severe Alzheimer's. She had saved a certain amount, not a lot; she had only about $200,000. It was not enough for Gloria to continue very long with the level of supervised care that she now required. My friend had turned to us once her mother was diagnosed. We knew the family was in for an unpleasant and painful journey. Gloria's family was going to have to do for her what many children of seniors have to do today. It's called a "spend down." For Gloria to qualify for a Medicare-approved memory facility, her savings had to be spent down to about $2,000. This amount varies from state to state, so you need to check for your situation.

While Gloria was still able to function at a relatively high cognitive level, her family sold Gloria's home and liquidated all of her assets. They moved her into a private residential memory care facility that had weekly game and entertainment nights, an activities center with a gym, a pool, and a massage therapist. They even had a card room with an open bar. The tab was $9,000 per month. In the three years that it took to spend down Gloria's assets, her condition

MORE LIFE THAN MONEY

had deteriorated to the point where she no longer recognized her family or even remembered her name. She no longer seemed aware that she had been moved into a government-funded facility, where she was given the same basic nursing care.

"I feel so guilty about her being there," said my friend. "But she doesn't know us from Adam."

That guilt is a heavy burden for your loved ones to bear. But had Gloria prepared in her younger years, the ending may have been different. Instead of being taken care of by the government at an approved facility, she may have been able to spend her final years in the comfort of her own home.

How do you prepare or pay for long-term care? Well, there are four ways. The first way is to self-insure. That's the default way. If you live in California, where I live, it could easily cost you over $100,000 a year to live in the standard, average nursing home facility. The second way is to qualify for government assistance. The third way is to purchase a traditional long-term care insurance policy. The final way is to invest in an asset-backed long-term care policy. Let's explore the pros and cons of each of these methods.

Dave's LTC Story

Dave is one of my best friends, and I use his story when I try to impress upon someone the fact that long-term care can be very expensive.

Dave had an aunt Edna and uncle Bill who had no children of their own and thought of Dave as a son. They recently passed away within a few months of each other at the age of ninety-four.

Dave told me the story of their lives. They both had good jobs and had invested wisely in real estate. When it came time to retire, they moved to Palm Springs and lived a comfortable lifestyle for many years, funding their retirement by selling off their properties over time. By the time they had reached their mideighties, their liquid net worth was close to $2 million. Around age eighty-nine, both started needing long-term care services within six months of each other. They asked Dave to take over their financial affairs with one caveat: he had to solemnly swear that he would keep them in their home and not send them to a nursing home.

Edna passed first. She had just turned ninety-four. Dave called me up after the funeral and asked for some advice. There was only about seven months' worth of liquid assets left in the estate. He was thinking of doing a reverse mortgage on their home and wanted to know my thoughts. It turned out that he didn't have to do anything.

Uncle Bill followed his beloved Edna just two months later.

The moral of the story is that Edna and Bill did not have LTC insurance. So, by default, they self-financed their care so they could stay in their home as long as possible. In the span of five years, they had gone through almost $2 million in order to do that.

If you want to stay at your home, then you have to be able to afford it. If you even want to consider self-insuring today, you had better begin with a net worth of at least $10 million, especially if you don't need it until a couple of decades from now when it's much more expensive. If you desire to leave a legacy, then protecting your estate from a catastrophic long-term care situation is a must.

Government Assistance Programs

The second way to pay for long-term care is through government assistance. As we've already discussed, the reality is that most people won't qualify for government programs without spending down nearly everything they have. Government assistance is really self-insuring until you become basically indigent, and then the government will pay for you. If you don't have a lot of means, this may be your only option. If you do have a decent-sized estate, you probably won't qualify.

Traditional Long-Term Care Insurance

The third way to pay for long-term care is through traditional long-term care (LTC) insurance. LTC coverage is offered by a limited number of insurance companies, and policies are subject to medical approval and vary by state. Almost all policies have exclusions, restrictions, limitations, and reductions in benefits that may apply in certain situations, and you need to make sure your financial services professional or insurance agent explains them so you truly understand your coverage. All guarantees are subject to the claims-paying ability of the underwriting company; if it goes out of business or becomes financially insolvent, your coverage could be affected.

It is standard practice for a minimum premium amount to be required. Premiums may be funded with a single premium or, depending on the product, paid annually, semiannually, quarterly, or monthly, along with a service fee. Some plans offer optional riders, and these usually have an additional premium.

The reason so few Americans have traditional long-term care insurance is because it's so expensive. If you're in your sixties today trying to get a long-term care insurance policy, a decent plan may cost you three to five hundred dollars a month per person. The good thing is that these policies can be custom built, and you can pay as little as fifty dollars a month for a cheap policy or up to $2,000 a month for a higher quality one.

There are a couple of things to note about LTC. The first is that the majority of LTC policies have end dates, and it's common to see policies that end after three or four years. If you're in a nursing home for ten years, only the first three or four years may be covered. Once the coverage ends, you'll fall back to being self-insured. If you're in a convalescent home for an extended period, you may still go broke, even if you had coverage for the first part of your stay.

Because you have no idea what the future holds, you may be one of the unlucky ones who ends up in a nursing home for a long time. And the only way to insure successfully is to make sure that you have coverage that lasts as long as you need it.

Another pitfall is that LTC insurance companies can raise the premiums. I sold some long-term care policies twenty years ago when I got into the business, but I didn't know what I know now. What I didn't know was that the insurance companies drastically underestimated how long people were going to live, and how many people were going to need long-term care, and they dramatically underpriced these long-term care policies. The sales pitch was, "Oh, they can't raise the premiums for you. They can only raise the premiums for an entire class of people."

Well, when the entire class of people gets to eighty or eighty-five years old, and they all start to need LTC, the insurance company is more than ecstatic to raise premiums for the entire class. In the last two or three years, I have had clients who have been priced out of LTC insurance because the premiums have skyrocketed. I had one client couple in their early eighties who told me that their LTC insurance premium went up 40 percent the previous year and 20 percent the year before that. That's a 60 percent increase in just two years. I had another client in her early seventies whose premium went up 40 percent last year.

Plus, traditional LTC policies are "use it or lose it" policies. You may pay your premiums for decades, and if you die in your sleep one night, as we all desire, you receive nothing for all the tens of thousands or more that you have paid. For these reasons, I often don't recommend traditional long-term care insurance, especially because there is a better way, which I will discuss next.

Asset-Backed Long-Term Care Insurance

The final way to pay for long-term care insurance is through asset-backed insurance. Essentially, this product is a combination of life insurance and long-term care insurance in one package. In the last two decades or so, life insurance companies have designed combination policies that not only pay a death benefit when you die but also pay a monthly long-term care benefit should you ever need it.

This allows you to take a sum of cash, often $100,000–$200,000, depending on your situation, and transfer that sum to an insurance company. Now, the most important thing to know about this transfer is that you're not spending the lump sum; you're just transferring it from one pocket to the other. The reason is that you can always get it back if you want to. It still stays on your balance sheet. It's still yours. It's almost as if you transferred funds from one bank to another; you can always transfer it back if you want to. The worst-case scenario is there may be a 2 to 5 percent surcharge if you transfer it back within the first decade or so. Transferring this cash to the insurance company provides you with two important benefits.

First, because it is a life insurance policy, you get a death benefit. You transfer the money to the insurance company, and they're going to give you a death benefit that will be distributed to your heirs when you die. And, as with all life insurance policies, the death benefit is tax-free.

The death benefit is going to be based on your age, health, and a number of other factors. The younger you are and the better your health, the more death benefit you get. If you're married, this policy is engineered as a joint life policy, also known as a second-to-die policy, so it only pays when the second person dies. This lowers the internal cost of insurance, because odds are one of you is going to live longer than the other.

The second benefit that they give you is that if you need long-term care down the road, they will accelerate the death benefit to you in the form of a monthly payment that can be used for the purpose of paying long-term care expenses.

We don't know for sure that you're ever going to need long-term care, but we can be fairly certain that you're going to die. If you die without ever using it to cover long-term care expenses, your beneficiaries will receive the death benefit.

These life-LTC combo products have evolved over the years, and I am a huge fan. Asset-backed insurance is a fairly new concept, and for the first time that I am aware of, you can use a retirement account to fund this type of policy.

Let's look at a couple of examples so you get an understanding of how they work.

Examples

Martha and Charlie are a married couple, both age sixty, nonsmoking professionals living in Laguna Beach, California. They pay an initial premium of $100,000 to the insurance company. This is the "asset" part of "asset-backed" long-term care. They are simply transferring the savings from one investment vehicle to the next, one pocket to the other. Their $100,000 stays on their balance sheet as an asset, and if they ever change their minds, they can always transfer the funds back as previously outlined. The table shown on the next page illustrates an initial premium of $100,000 transferred to an asset-backed insurance policy. The first item to note is that the policy provides a death benefit of $194,621. Therefore, when the second spouse dies, this benefit will pass to their beneficiaries tax-free if they never used it for long-term care.

LONG-TERM CARE BENEFITS IF TAKEN AT AGE 60	
Total Initial Premium:	$100,000
Death Benefit:	$194,621
Total LTC Benefit Balance/Benefit Periods:	Unlimited/Lifetime
Initial Premium:	$100,000
Death Benefit:	$194,621
Total LTC Benefit Balance:	
Death Benefits — Pays for LTC	Unlimited
Initial LTC Benefit Limit, Per Individual:	$5,838 Monthly
	$70,056 Annually
Initial LTC Benefit Limit, For One	$11,676 Monthly
Or Both Individual:	($5,838 per Person)
	$140,112 Annually
	($70,056 per Person)

Source: One America Care Solutions Calculator, https://www.oneamerica.com//caresolutionscalculator/index.html.

TABLE G

The second component is that it also provides a long-term care benefit of up to $5,838 per month for one spouse and up to $11,676 per month if both spouses need coverage simultaneously. When you start using this benefit, the first dollars that the insurance company is spending on your behalf will be deducted from the death benefit.

The most important benefit of this kind of policy is that it comes with a feature (called a continuation of benefits rider) that provides ongoing protection once you've blown through the death benefit.

There is a cost for this rider, and in this example, the premium is only $1,794 per year for the couple. If you have ever shopped for traditional long-term care insurance, you know that this is only a fraction of what you would spend with a traditional long-term care insurance policy with the same benefits. This premium begins when the initial coverage begins and cannot be increased by the insurance company. That is true financial peace of mind: unlimited coverage at $5,838 per month per person for long-term care until you die or no longer need it with a guarantee that your premium will never increase.

The longer you wait, the more expensive the LTC coverage gets. Let's look at what would happen if Martha and Charlie waited until they were seventy-five to take out this same policy.

This illustration (shown on the next page) shows that they have kept the initial premium the same, but the death benefit and the LTC benefits are considerably less, because they are fifteen years older. The death benefit decreases by more than $75,000, and the monthly LTC benefit drops by more than $2,200 per month per person. Quite a decrease. And to make matters worse, the premium for the continuation of benefits rider has gone up over $1,200 per year.

More importantly, if one of the spouse's health has deteriorated between the time they were sixty and seventy-five years old, they may not even be able to get coverage at all, because there are minimum health requirements to qualify.

LONG-TERM CARE BENEFITS IF TAKEN AT AGE 75	
Total Initial Premium:	$99,999
Death Benefit:	$119,300
Total LTC Benefit Balance/Benefit Periods:	Unlimited/Lifetime
Initial Premium:	$99,999
Death Benefit:	$119,300
Total LTC Benefit Balance:	
Death Benefits — Pays for LTC	Unlimited
Initial LTC Benefit Limit, Per Individual:	$3,578 Monthly
	$42,936 Annually
Initial LTC Benefit Limit, For One	$7,156 Monthly
Or Both Individual:	($3,578 per Person)
	$85,872 Annually
	($42,936 per Person)

Source: One America Care Solutions Calculator, https://www.oneamerica.
com//caresolutionscalculator/index.html.

TABLE H

There's a saying in the insurance industry: it is your health that buys insurance—the money only pays for it. The sooner you get coverage, the better.

> *There's a saying in the insurance industry: it is your health that buys insurance–the money only pays for it.*

By now I hope you can see why I like these types of policies. You get a death benefit if you die without ever using the long-term care feature. The cost is much less than an equivalent traditional long-term care policy, and the premium is guaranteed to never increase. Because of these guarantees, you can rest assured that you will have the coverage when you need it—you will not be priced out.

If one of the goals is to stay at home should you ever need long-term care and to leave a legacy to the next generation, it is something worth looking into.

CHAPTER SEVEN

What You Don't Know about Social Security

"An act to provide for the general welfare by establishing a system of Federal old-age benefits, and by enabling the several States to make more adequate provision for aged persons, blind persons, dependent and crippled children, maternal and child welfare, public health, and the administration of their unemployment compensation laws; to establish a Social Security Board; to raise revenue; and for other purposes.

Be it enacted by the Senate and House of Representatives of the United States of America in Congress assembled."

—THE SOCIAL SECURITY ACT (ACT OF
AUGUST 14, 1935) [H. R. 7260]

That is the preamble to the 1935 legislation that gave birth to what is now keeping more than 40 percent of retirees out of poverty: namely, Social Security income.

What You Need To Know

You can go to socialsecurity.gov and create a free account and download your statement. Your statement will give you an idea about how much you will get if you retire at a certain age. I do workshops and webinars strictly about Social Security. The decision on how and when to take Social Security is absolutely critical; and yet, I find that most people don't take a lot of time in deciding when to take Social Security. I've conversed with hundreds of people who have told me they got their information from reading a magazine article or talking with a friend or coworker. They will ask that person, "When are you going to take it?" or, "What do you think?" as if the individual somehow knows more than they do about this complex program. It is one of the most important decisions that you'll ever make, yet too many people still decide when to take their Social Security benefits based on fiction, not fact. The sad reality is that many of them are leaving thousands of dollars of retirement income on the table.

Several years ago, I had a professional couple in their midsixties who had come to one of our Social Security workshops. He was an attorney, and she was an executive at a Fortune 500 company. They were both well-educated and very bright people. They were curious about something I had said in the seminar.

"I'm an attorney," said the husband. "I know how to do research, and I have not found anything like the strategy you shared in the seminar."

They had asked me to run a computer simulation for them. The strategy that I had shared was worth $48,000 to them. It was $48,000 of lost income over a four-year period of time that they would never have collected had they taken their benefits as they were intending. What they didn't know about Social Security was worth $48,000 to them. They would not have collected any of that money had they not met with me before determining when to take their benefits.

Here's the bottom line. From a purely mathematical analysis, there's only one right way and one wrong way to take Social Security. We measure the right and wrong way based on lifetime benefits assuming you live to a certain age. Our Social Security software defaults to the assumption that both parties die at ninety-three years old. Some live longer, and some don't make it that far. We run a worst-case versus best-case scenario of when to begin taking your benefits, showing married couples the difference between lifetime benefits and the best and the worst way of taking Social Security benefits. The differences are staggering.

Generally speaking, the best time to file for benefits is at age seventy; but there are exceptions. If you are sixty-five years old and don't have a job and can't afford to wait until seventy, then you do what you have to do. If you are in bad health and may not be around that long, it may be best to file earlier. Those are pieces of your puzzle that we need to know before making a recommendation.

There are some other things you should know about Social Security. The first thing is that it doesn't matter who you are: the benefits are calculated the same way. The second thing is that it's all based around average life expectancies.

When you do the calculations, you'll see that your Social Security benefits will break even somewhere around eighty years old. That is the point where you will have collected the same amount of cumulative benefits regardless of whether you filed at sixty-two or seventy or somewhere in between.

MORE LIFE THAN MONEY

Determining Your Benefit

How does the Social Security Administration determine what your monthly Social Security benefit will be at full retirement age? The amount of your benefit is based on a formula that takes into consideration your thirty-five highest years of earnings. They take the thirty-five highest years of earnings and index them for inflation. They do this because what you made thirty-five years ago is not going to be the same or anywhere near what you earn today in terms of real dollars, so they bring everything to a current number and come up with something called average indexed monthly earnings (AIME). They then run your AIME through a complex formula, based upon the changes in the national wage index over those same earnings years, which gives them the sum of three separate percentages of portions of average indexed monthly earnings. The formula as of 2019 is as follows:

- 90 percent of the first $926 of his/her average indexed monthly earnings, plus

- 32 percent of his/her average indexed monthly earnings over $926 and through $5,583, plus

- 15 percent of his/her average indexed monthly earnings over $5,583.[26]

The result is called your primary insurance amount (PIA). The PIA is the amount of benefit you get at your full retirement age (FRA) which is the age at which you will collect the full amount based on your previous earnings. If you choose to take it early, you will receive a reduced amount, whereas if you delay filing until seventy, you will

---

26   The Motley Fool, "What's the Social Security Benefit Formula?," August 23, 2019, https://www.fool.com/retirement/whats-the-social-security-benefit-formula.aspx.

collect more. You can start taking your Social Security benefit as early as age sixty-two, but it will be about 30 percent less than if you wait until your full retirement age and considerably less than if you waited until age seventy.

It Pays To Wait

It is important that you understand the concept of full retirement age. The full retirement age is going to depend on what year you were born. Here is what you need to know about your full retirement age.

If you take your Social Security benefit early, then you get penalized. If you take it later, you get a bonus.

Absent an exception, the earliest you can take Social Security is sixty-two. The latest that you want to wait to take Social Security is seventy. There's no increase in benefits for waiting beyond seventy. If you were born between 1943 and 1954, your full retirement age is sixty-six, and that is when you would get 100 percent of your primary insurance amount. You could start taking your monthly benefit as early as sixty-two; but if your full retirement age is sixty-six, then at sixty-two you'll get about 30 percent less. If you can wait until age seventy to start receiving your Social Security benefits, your monthly benefit will be 32 percent higher than at age sixty-six. Remember, once you start taking your monthly benefit, that is normally the amount you will receive, plus cost-of-living increases, until your death. As you will see later, there is usually an exception to almost every rule when it comes to government programs.

Your full retirement age is sixty-six if you were born from 1943 to 1954. The full retirement age increases gradually if you were born from 1955 to 1960 until it reaches sixty-seven. For anyone born 1960 or later, full retirement benefits are payable at age sixty-seven. The following chart lists the full retirement age by year of birth.

AGE TO RECEIVE FULL SOCIAL SECURITY BENEFITS	
Year of Birth	**Full Retirement Age**
1943–1954	66
1955	66 and 2 Months
1956	66 and 4 Months
1957	66 and 6 Months
1958	66 and 8 Months
1959	66 and 10 Months
1960 And Later	67
Note: People born on January 1st of any year, refer to the previous year	

Source: Social Security, "Retirement Benefits," https://www.ssa.gov/benefits/retirement/planner/agereduction.html.

TABLE I

Let's say Rocky O'Hare was born June 1, 1957. That would make his full retirement age sixty-six and six months. It is 2019, and he just turned sixty-two. If the monthly benefit at his full FRA was $1,000, and he decided to take his benefit at age sixty-two, he would only receive 72.5 percent of his FRA benefit. That is $725. It is reduced because he will be getting benefits for an additional fifty-four months.

O'Hare's neighbor, Tonya Tortoise, is the same age, but she decides to wait until she's seventy to take her Social Security. By waiting to age seventy, her benefit increased to 128 percent of the FRA monthly benefit to $1,280 per month, because she delayed getting benefits for forty-two months.

There will, of course, be those "armchair experts" who will point out that by taking it at age sixty-two, O'Hare would have made $69,600 before Tortoise ever filed. That is true, but by waiting until age seventy, Tortoise will have collected $153,600 by age eighty. The quick starter O'Hare, even with the eight-year head start, would have collected only $3,000 more. By age eighty-two, O'Hare will be behind by $10,320, and the gap between him and Tortoise will continue to grow every year thereafter.

With advancements in medicine and the trend toward a healthier lifestyle, people are living considerably longer today than their parents did. By age ninety, Ms. Tortoise will have received $307,200. That is $63,600 more than O'Hare. Bottom line: it pays to wait.

The Spousal Benefit

The Social Security spousal benefit is another important one to understand. Social Security was started in 1935, when we were still a very patriarchal society. A lot of the women stayed home maintaining the household and raising the children, which is a lot of work without a paycheck. Things are very different today, and women work as much as men. In many situations, the wife makes more than the husband, and in some cases the husband stays home to take care of the children.

As an example, let's say that a husband has a PIA of $2,500 at his full retirement age. The spousal benefit says that if the wife's benefit is less than one-half of the husband's PIA, then the wife is entitled to at least one-half of the husband's primary insurance amount. One-half of the husband's PIA, in this example, would be $1,250. The wife would be entitled to that monthly benefit even if she's never paid a dime into Social Security and even while the husband is collecting his full PIA.

The Widow's Benefit

Another benefit from Social Security that is often overlooked is the widow's benefit. This benefit says that when you're married and one spouse passes away, the surviving spouse is going to have the opportunity to keep their own benefit or switch over to the deceased's larger Social Security benefit. While many spouses are aware of this provision, they often fail to plan for the fact that, upon the demise of the first spouse, the second spouse is going to lose the smaller Social Security benefit. Plus, the surviving spouse's taxes will likely go up because they are now a single filer. Reduction of income plus higher taxes equals a disgruntled surviving spouse, which is why you must plan for this. If you were married for over ten years and your ex-spouse died, then you can get their Social Security, provided you did not remarry before age sixty. If you remarry after you reach age sixty (age fifty if disabled), the remarriage will not affect your eligibility for survivor's benefits. There can also be more than one person collecting Social Security benefits on your ex. Benefits paid to you as a surviving divorced spouse won't affect the benefit amount for other survivors getting benefits on the worker's record.

If you are caring for a child under age sixteen *or* for a child who is disabled, you could also get benefits on the record of your former spouse without meeting the ten-year length-of-marriage rule. The child must be your former spouse's natural or legally adopted child.

The Divorced Spouse Benefit

Next is the divorce spousal benefit. If you were married for a minimum of ten years before you divorced, you can file for half of your ex-spouse's PIA. Or your ex-spouse could file and collect half of your PIA. It sounds like the proverbial "gift that keeps on giving," but don't worry. Neither spouse will ever know that their ex has filed for the benefit, because it doesn't have any effect on the primary beneficiary.

But there are a few rules. You can receive benefits on your ex-spouse's record (even if they have remarried) if you, the ex-spouse, were married for at least ten years, are currently unmarried, and are age sixty-two or older; your ex-spouse is entitled to Social Security retirement or disability benefits; and your own benefit is less than what you would receive from the divorced spousal benefit. Also, the benefits do not include any delayed retirement credits your ex-spouse may receive.

When I told a friend of mine about this benefit, he went off on a rant about the far-reaching consequences of the government's largesse.

"So, if I understand you correctly," he said sarcastically, "I graduated at twenty-six after attaining my MBA and married my college sweetheart. I did quite well in my profession but had personal commitment issues that caused me to divorce and remarry every ten years. By the time I reached sixty-seven and filed for my full benefit of $4,000 per month, you are telling me that I would be providing an opportunity for each of my five ex-wives to claim a divorced spousal benefit of $2,000 per month?" Yep!

The "Sand Traps" Of Social Security

One of the myths of Social Security is that unless you are disabled, you receive it only after you stop working. That isn't true. You can still work after you start collecting your Social Security benefit; but, like sand traps on your favorite golf course, there are some provisions you must be aware of so that you can successfully navigate past them.

You can work while you are receiving Social Security benefits, and for each year that you do, the government will use those earnings to recalculate your PIA. This could actually lead to an increase in the amount of your benefit over and above any cost-of-living adjustments.

If you are younger than your full retirement age and still working, your benefit will be reduced one dollar for every two dollars earned above the annual limit. That limit is $18,960 for 2021;[27] the SSA website will have the current limit. In reference to this particular benefit reduction, "earnings" are defined as wages paid to you by your employer, or your net profit if you're self-employed, plus any bonuses, commissions, and vacation pay. Passive income you receive from any pensions, annuities, investment income, interest, and veterans' or other government or military retirement benefits are excluded.

In the year that you reach your full retirement age, the formula and the limit change. In 2021, one dollar is deducted for every three dollars earned above the limit of $50,250, but only on earnings before the month you reach full retirement age. Once you reach full retirement age, your benefit is no longer reduced, regardless of the amount of your earnings. As long as you continue to work, your record will be recalculated to determine if the new earnings increase your monthly benefit. If it does, your Social Security benefit will increase as a result.

It is easy to think of the reduction of benefits due to earnings as a penalty, but it isn't. After you reach full retirement age, SSA will recalculate your monthly benefit and credit you the amount that your benefit was reduced due to earnings before FRA. It will be, on the average, fifteen years before you realize the full return on the credit. So why does Social Security reduce your benefit if they are just going to give it back to you? That is like asking why your Social Security benefits are taxed. It is another one of those "sand traps" you need to know about.

---

27   Social Security Administration, "How Much Can I Earn and Still Get Benefits?,"
      https://www.ssa.gov/benefits/retirement/planner/whileworking.html#:~:text=If%20
      you%20are%20under%20full,earn%20above%20a%20different%20limit.

Additionally, if you are receiving Social Security benefits before your FRA, and you earn more than the applicable limit for the year, there is another trap you need to be cautious of. Social Security does not know how much you're going to earn that year—or that you're even working. Therefore, don't expect them to deduct the amount you owe them every month. Instead, Social Security will not find out how much you owe them until you file your taxes the following year. If you've made too much money, not only will you have to pay taxes, but you'll also have to reimburse the Social Security Administration for the excess amount you received. Although this reimbursement is not a penalty in the true sense of the word, it will feel like one when you have to write that check. You also have to be prepared for additional taxes when you begin receiving Social Security.

If you make too much money while you are collecting Social Security benefits, the IRS will take your Social Security benefits and add half of it in with the other income you receive from pensions, annuities, interest, dividends, and wages. They call this "provisional income." Moreover, all of that "nontaxable" municipal bond interest you are receiving counts toward your provisional income. For example, if you are married, filing jointly, and your "provisional income" is over $34,000, you could end up having to pay taxes on half of your Social Security benefits. If you are a single filer and your provisional income is between $25,000 and $34,000, 50 percent of your benefits could be taxed. Furthermore, if you're single and your provisional income is over $42,000, or if you're married and filing jointly and your provisional income exceeds $44,000, you will have to pay taxes on up to 85 percent of your Social Security.

I refer you to IRS Publication 915, *Social Security and Equivalent Railroad Retirement Benefits*, for a much more detailed explanation of the taxation of retirement benefits. I would also encourage you to pay attention to your mailbox in January if you are receiving Social Security benefits. The SSA sends out a document called a Social Security Benefit Statement (Form SSA-1099), which will show the amount of benefits you received in the previous year. Take this benefit statement with you when you have your taxes done. Your CPA will need it to determine if your benefits are subject to tax.

Conclusion

As I said in the beginning of this chapter, Social Security is a complex issue, and we have only hit the highlights. I urge you to do yourself a favor and go online to https://www.ssa.gov/ and sign up. Explore the website and learn as much as you can. Alternatively, talk to your financial advisor and have him or her explain the potential sand traps and how you may benefit from these rules. You have worked hard and earned this benefit. Make sure you know what you have coming to you and how best to take it, because what you don't know about Social Security can cause you to leave thousands of dollars in Uncle Sam's account.

CHAPTER EIGHT

What You Don't Know about Annuities

ONE OF THE biggest fears I hear about is the fear of outliving one's assets. The industry term for this is *longevity risk*. It is not an irrational fear. Social Security was designed to help deal with longevity risk, as were pension plans that had defined lifetime benefits. These two are examples of an "annuity."

What Is An Annuity?

An annuity, in its purest form, is a stream of income made at equal intervals. An individual, the annuitant, receives a series of payments or an "income stream" from Social Security or from their pension plan. When a person wins a large settlement in a lawsuit, those payments are structured usually in monthly payments over a period of years to create an income stream. When the lottery pays a jackpot winner *X* millions of dollars in periodic payments over twenty years, they are creating an income stream for the winner. These are all examples of annuities.

An annuity can be created for an individual retirement account (IRA), or it can be a non-IRA. The distinction is in the treatment of taxes. Traditional IRA contributions are tax deductible on both state and federal tax returns for the year you make the contribution. Upon retirement, withdrawals are taxed as ordinary income for the life of the annuity.

For a nonretirement annuity, the contribution is made with after-tax money and allowed to grow tax deferred. When you begin taking withdrawals from a non-IRA annuity, only the earned interest portion is taxed. Once the withdrawals use up the earned interest, withdrawals are no longer taxed.

There are two broad categories of annuities: immediate and deferred. An immediate annuity converts the funds invested into a series of periodic income payments for the life of the recipient or for a predetermined specified period of time. This type of annuity is called an immediate annuity, because you begin to receive payments immediately after you purchase it. It is the equivalent of buying a pension. You give the insurance company a lump sum of money, and in return they provide monthly payments that are guaranteed to last as long as you are alive, for a specified period of time, or a combination of both. More on this to follow.

On the other hand, a deferred annuity is often used more as a savings or investment vehicle. Although this type of annuity allows you to exchange the principal for a guaranteed periodic payment, it does not require that you do so. Therefore, you can purchase a deferred annuity and, at some point in the future, withdraw your entire investment as a lump sum if you want.

All annuities are contracts with an insurance company. The initial premium is most often a lump-sum amount, usually transferred from savings or other investment vehicles, or you can fund it through a series of annual or monthly premium payments. Don't let the word *premium* confuse you. Because only insurance companies offer annuities, they use insurance terms, including the term *premium*, which is just another way of saying initial deposit or investment.

In most cases, an individual will deposit a lump sum into the annuity and never make another contribution. The insurance company may allow you to contribute more into your annuity if you want to, depending on the terms of that specific annuity. You are never required to add any more money to it if you don't want to. Because it is an annuity, it offers you the option of exchanging the lump sum for a guaranteed income stream down the road if you so desire. Most people simply purchase the annuity, let it perform the way it is structured to perform, and then either cash it out at some future date or bequeath it to their beneficiaries.

There are multiple types of annuities based upon funding, building value, and paying out benefits. One of the most attractive features of nonretirement annuities is that contributions are tax deferred. When you contribute funds to an annuity with after-tax dollars, the interest or growth is tax deferred; you are not required to pay tax on the growth until you make a withdrawal. This allows you, not the government, to determine when you pay the tax.

An annuity is not right for everyone, but it is a great way to save money in a conservative investment, and it is a very good way to get lifetime income, if that is your goal. You should also be careful who you buy the annuity from. There are a lot of annuity salespeople out there who sell them strictly for commissions, and they don't understand how they work. If you buy an annuity that is not right for you, at best you'll find yourself in a contract that pays very little interest, and at worst you'll lose a lot of money while paying hefty fees.

I've been an annuity expert for over two decades, and I can honestly say that it probably took me a good eight or ten years to truly understand the ins and outs of how they work. As a tool in the hands of a professional who knows the finer details, they can be a valuable addition to someone's retirement plan. In the hands of an inexperienced life insurance agent solely looking to make a sale, they can be a big mistake.

The Four Basic Types Of Annuities

Broadly speaking, an annuity can be classified into one of four categories, depending on how it generates returns for the owner:

- The Immediate Annuity

- The Fixed Annuity

- The Index Annuity

- The Variable Annuity

THE IMMEDIATE ANNUITY

As mentioned previously, an immediate annuity allows you to exchange a lump sum for a steady stream of income. This "steady stream of income" can be paid to you monthly or over a specified period of time. The "defined period" can be the lifetime of the recipient, a specified number of years, until a certain age, or until the benefits are exhausted. It can begin at a certain age or some other triggering event like retirement or death of a spouse.

You can set up an annuity that will pay you every month for ten, twenty, or thirty years. If you pick a longer period, you will get a smaller payment. If you set up a twenty-year annuity, it's going to pay 240 payments to you or whomever you choose as the beneficiary should you pass away before the end of that twenty-year phase.

You can set up an annuity that is a combination of the two. The insurance company will guarantee the payments will continue as long as you're alive *or* until they have made payments for a specified number of years, whichever is longer. It is important to understand that most of the time when you add a feature to your annuity, you get less monthly income as a result.

Let's look at a hypothetical example: Mike, who is seventy years old, is a retiring account executive living in a home on the golf course in Winnetka, Illinois. Although he had a very successful career, he was an independent contractor. He contributed to Social Security but didn't have a company pension. When he retires, he's going to need extra income. He and his wife, Shirley, who is also seventy, sell the Chicagoland home and downsize to a condo on the golf course in Bradenton, Florida.

Because they downsized, they have $300,000 left over that they plan on using to provide income for the rest of their lives. They can give this lump sum to a highly rated insurance company in exchange for an immediate annuity. Mike wants to have a fixed monthly payment that will last as long as he does, but should he die first, he also wants that monthly income to continue for as long as Shirley is alive. One such highly rated insurance company will issue Mike an immediate annuity that will guarantee a monthly income of $1,514.82 for as long as either he or his wife is breathing.

In this example, if either Mike or Shirley lives to be eighty-six, they will have broken even. If one of them lives to be ninety-five, the annuity will have paid out over $450,000 in monthly payments. Should one of them live to be a centenarian, the insurance company will have paid out over $545,000 to the couple. The power of the immediate annuity in this example is that the payments are guaranteed to last for their lifetime.

Sounds good, right? Not so fast; there are some significant drawbacks to this example. First, an immediate annuity is irrevocable, and even if you need the money later on, once you purchase it and hand over the lump sum, there is no turning back.

Another downside is that your beneficiaries may not receive anything following your death. If you die before receiving all of your money back, the insurance company may keep the remaining balance.

You might ask why someone would ever purchase an immediate annuity. One of the primary reasons would be for the favorable tax benefits. If you've had a deferred annuity (to be discussed later) that has grown substantially over the years, there is potentially a huge tax consequence if you cash out. If you use those funds to buy an immediate annuity, the taxes will be prorated proportionally with each payment, thereby providing you guaranteed income with a significant reduction in tax.

Let's use another example to illustrate the tax benefits. Charles is seventy-five and Colleen is seventy. Fifteen years ago, they purchased an annuity for $150,000, which has since doubled. Because annuities are tax deferred, they have never paid taxes on the $150,000 they gained. If they decide to cash out, that gain will be taxed as ordinary income, which will generate quite a hefty tax bill. But if they simply choose to buy an immediate annuity with the $300,000, their taxes will be substantially reduced.

Because they are concerned about losing the entire principal should they both die prematurely, they decide to set up an immediate annuity that will pay them for as long as either one of them is living or for fifteen years, whichever is longer. In this scenario, a highly rated insurance company will provide them with an income stream of $1,531 per month. The insurance company guarantees that they will receive these payments for at least fifteen years or until the second of them dies, whichever is longer. Best of all, because they have already paid taxes on the $150,000 they originally contributed to the annuity, only $916 of each monthly payment will be taxed. This allows them to maximize their monthly income while minimizing their taxes, something they could not do if they simply cashed their annuity in.

If they both pass away before the insurance company has made 180 monthly payments (fifteen years), the remaining payments will be made to their beneficiaries. Under this scenario, the insurance company guarantees to pay out at least $275,580 worth of benefits, thereby making this the worst-case scenario. If Colleen lives to be one hundred, then the insurance company would have paid out over $550,000 of payments.

Besides the tax benefits, another reason people may purchase an immediate annuity is because they are worried they'll spend the principal they have access to. That this type of annuity is irrevocable is a significant benefit, because it provides them with the peace of mind of knowing that they can't touch the principal and, at the same time, can't outlive the income. Although not common, I've had clients who can't control their spending habits, and an immediate annuity is one way to protect them from themselves.

Additionally, and more commonly, some retirees are worried that their kids or grandchildren will spend all the money. To combat this, an annuity can be set up so that it will provide a guaranteed lifetime income stream to the next generation while making sure that the beneficiaries cannot access the principal in a lump sum.

Yet another reason that some professionals purchase an immediate annuity is because they are worried about getting sued.

Because exchanging a lump sum for a lifetime income is an irrevocable contract, the principal cannot be accessed by creditors.

But you have to be careful: if you set up an annuity with fraudulent intent, the court may still order the contract to be broken in order to pay your creditors.

I often recommend against using an immediate annuity because of the severe restriction of being irrevocable and the potential of losing your principal if you die early. Although there are times when it makes sense, there are often better ways to get the same income without having to relinquish control of the principal.

The immediate annuity is the only type that is irrevocable and causes you to give up access to your funds. The other types of annuities discussed next allow you to remain in control with full flexibility to withdraw all of your funds at a later date.

FIXED ANNUITY

A fixed annuity is the easiest annuity to understand, because it's going to pay you a fixed rate of return, guaranteed by the issuing company. It's similar to a certificate of deposit issued by a bank or credit union in that you know how much interest you will earn over a period of time.

There are some fixed annuities that will guarantee you a specific interest rate for just one year but give you the ability to readjust the interest every year. Other fixed annuities will guarantee you an interest rate for a specific period, usually three to five years—sometimes longer. Your principal is 100 percent protected, subject to the claims-paying ability of the insurance company, which is why you want to be with a solid company.

The insurance company commingles your investment with their general account just like a bank does. You have no control over how your funds are invested, but you do know the rate of return you're going to get, because it is fixed. This may be a good investment for someone who is allergic to risk, because you will likely earn more than the bank, while having tax-deferred growth and a guaranteed investment.

VARIABLE ANNUITY

The variable annuity allows you to invest in a pool of "subaccounts" that you usually get to select based upon your investing strategy and your personal risk tolerance. These subaccounts look and feel a lot like mutual funds, and they may even be called mutual funds; but insurance companies call them subaccounts when they are put into a variable annuity.

The challenge with variable annuities, though, is that many people, often including the salespeople who sell them, don't understand how they work. I believe that if they did, most people would not buy them—for three reasons. First, you are shouldering all of the risk of loss; second, they have ginormous fees; and third, even though they are invested in subaccounts that are subject to capital appreciation, the interest you earn is subject to ordinary income tax, not capital gains tax, which is often more favorable. Let's dig deeper on each of these drawbacks.

First, when you purchase a variable annuity, the risk of loss is on you. Most of the times when I meet with someone who has a variable annuity, they are not aware of this. Your return will be based upon how the subaccounts in your annuity perform. You may make or lose money, and you are the one taking the risk, not the insurance company.

Second, variable annuities have high fees. I've often seen these fees reach unreasonably high levels, commonly in the 3 to 4 percent range annually. If you have $200,000 in a variable annuity with a 3 percent fee, you'll pay $6,000 per year for the privilege of accepting all the risk. If you hold the annuity for a decade, you may pay $60,000 or more in fees.

One of the worst examples I've seen recently was this couple who came to me because they were concerned about their annuity. Over time, they had seen a gain of $75,000 across their subaccounts, but all of the transaction fees, management fees, and rider fees totaled $78,000. It was perfectly legal, but it was hardly set up to be in their best interest as investors. This couple was accepting 100 percent of the risk but sharing all the profits equally with the insurance company. Sounds like a good deal for the insurance company.

Third, variable annuities are not tax efficient. All gains from a variable annuity are taxed as ordinary income, not capital gains, as they would be if you invested in similar mutual funds outside of the annuity. Because annuities tax you on a last-in, first-out basis, when you begin taking income from your annuity, you will pay ordinary income tax on all your income until you have spent down all the gains.

There is one benefit, however, that most variable annuities offer: they usually have a death benefit provided at no cost. The typical variable annuity death benefit clause states that if your money loses value, your beneficiaries will at least receive the amount of the contributions you made to fund the annuity. This can be a form of backstop if you want to be a bit riskier while protecting your beneficiaries. There is one main drawback, though: you have to die to guarantee that you'll get your principal back!

I generally avoid saying whether any investment is good or bad. I think that all investments may be good or bad *for you* depending on your life's situation and your money goals. An investment may be a perfect fit for one person and totally inappropriate for the next person. The variable annuity, however, is one investment I've never recommended, not once in my career.

From the negative tax ramifications, the fee structure, and the risk, in my opinion, you would be better off investing directly in mutual funds. While you do get some guarantees, I don't believe they are worth the fees and commissions.

INDEXED ANNUITY

A deviation on the variable annuity is the indexed annuity. Instead of a group of subaccounts, the insurance company puts your money into their general fund, which then gets invested per a lot of government regulations with specific criteria about what they can and cannot invest in. This usually means that they invest heavily in bonds and real estate.

I often describe an indexed annuity as being a hybrid between a variable annuity and a fixed annuity. Like a variable annuity, you can participate in the upside potential of the market. Like a fixed annuity, your principal is protected from loss. As a result, an index annuity is protected from the wild fluctuations of the variable, because you are not invested in the market; rather, you are simply tying your interest to an index. This acts as a floor or a sort of built-in "stop-loss" should the market take a significant downturn. The insurance company may lose money, but your principal is protected.

The interest you earn is not a set rate of return like it is with a fixed annuity. Instead, it is strictly dependent on how the stock market performs. Different annuity companies use different indexes, but many annuities tie your returns to one of the more common indexes, such as the Dow Jones or the S&P 500.

If your index goes up, you can capture some of the index's returns. The gains are split in some proportion with the annuity provider. If the stock market goes down, you do not make any interest, but you also do not lose any principal. The potential of not making interest in a year is the trade-off for the insurance company protecting your principal during a market downturn. Historically, from what I've seen over my career, insurance companies have often paid back between 25 percent and 50 percent of what the market has done.

People who are attracted to indexed annuities are those who like the idea of having a potentially higher return while feeling like they are participating in the stock market, but they don't want to risk their principal. I often tell people who are looking into the world of equities that there are bears, bulls, and chickens. An indexed annuity is for chickens.

RIDERS

Annuities are contracts and can have special clauses, known as "riders," attached to them. A rider is a clause or an additional document that adds or removes certain specified provisions of the subject contract. Most deferred annuities—fixed, index, or variable—give you the option to add riders onto them. Some come with a cost, while others do not. Whether you add on a rider that has an expense depends on the features of the rider.

Some of the typical riders that are added to annuities include the following:

- *Terminal illness* rider is for persons who are diagnosed with a terminal illness that lowers their life expectancy to a year or less. This rider will allow you access to your annuity or some portion thereof without having to pay the surrender fee.

- *Long-term care/nursing home* rider covers you if you need long-term care or you're confined to a nursing home for a certain period, usually sixty to ninety days. The insurance company will give you access to a certain portion of your money without a penalty. This is often 50 percent but could, depending upon the annuity, be 100 percent.

- *Cost of living* is a rider that increases the amount of your income payment to adjust for inflation but usually will start you with a lower initial payment amount or will have a cap on the increase.

- *Guaranteed lifetime withdrawal benefit* allows the owner to periodically withdraw a specified percentage of the amassed contributions until the annuity is exhausted. Note: this rider is only available on variable annuities and often has very complicated terms and conditions attached. Make sure your advisor fully and clearly explains the pros and cons of this rider. It is usually not worth the hassle.

- *Lifetime income benefit* is probably the most common rider because it can be added to either fixed, indexed, or variable annuities and guarantees a specified payment for the life of the owner or the joint lives of the owner and the spouse. Most often, the income rider gives you two guarantees. The first is that at some point down the road, you can start getting monthly income from your annuity. The amount of income you get is going to be based on actuarial tables and your life expectancy. The amount of income you receive depends on how old you are and on how long you let the money sit in the annuity before taking income. The insurance company projects how long you are going to live and how long you should be able to draw a specified monthly income from your annuity. If you live long enough, even though you have depleted all the money in your annuity, the insurance company is going to ensure that you keep receiving those monthly income payments for as long as you live. If you pass away before spending the entire principal, whatever is left will still go to your beneficiaries. The income can also be set up as a joint and survivor benefit so that the monthly income is guaranteed for you and your spouse as long as either of you is alive. This is one rider I feel is worth the price if you are relatively healthy and need income that is guaranteed to last as long as you're breathing.

The second guarantee of the lifetime income benefit rider is that for every year you delay taking income, the amount of income you get the following year is going to grow. Different companies grow at different rates, but generally speaking, your income will grow by between 5 percent and 7 percent a year. That serves as a hedge against inflation, so you are not sacrificing your spending power. There are some annuities that will start you off at a lower amount, but then they adjust for inflation over time. Some may have a systematic way of adjusting your income so it continues to get a little bit bigger every month instead of just being the same amount for as long as you live. Yes, there is a fee, but it mitigates the fear that people have of outliving their money.

Myths About Annuities

"MY MONEY IS LOCKED UP FOREVER."

A lot of people think that when you put money into an annuity, you don't get it back. As we've already discussed, that's only true for an immediate annuity. For the fixed, variable, or indexed varieties, you can withdraw your money anytime and for any reason you want; however, if you withdraw your money before the surrender charge period ends, then there could be a penalty. The surrender charge period varies from annuity to annuity, but I shy away from annuities that have a surrender charge period of more than ten years.

Most annuities give you access to a penalty-free withdrawal every year as long as the withdrawal is no more than 10 percent of the contract value. That amount varies with each provider, so make sure you read the terms and conditions of your annuity carefully when you set it up. Once the surrender period ends, your annuity is forever available to you with no penalty.

If you take out the money before age fifty-nine and a half, there may be an IRS penalty. That's true for both IRA and non-IRA annuities; however, there are exceptions to that. I had a client in her early fifties who developed serious health problems and was allowed to pull all of her investment out over time without a penalty. That is just one example. There are others, so you must have an advisor who knows how annuities work and knows the tax rules.

"WHEN I DIE, THE INSURANCE COMPANY KEEPS THE MONEY."

Again, this is only true with immediate annuities. It is not true with fixed, indexed, or variable annuities. Most annuities, other than the immediate annuity, allow your beneficiaries access to the entire value of the annuity plus any interest that it's earned with no penalty—even if you die before the surrender charge period has passed.

"THERE ARE SIGNIFICANT PENALTIES TO GET OUT."

Some annuities have a penalty that starts at less than 8 percent in the first year and then declines over time until the end of the surrender fee period. After that, there's no penalty at all.

If you have your money invested in a mutual fund, and you want to get out of your mutual fund at some point down the road, do you know the amount of the maximum loss you will take on that mutual fund? Not likely. If you buy a stock, do you know what the maximum loss is that you will take on that stock at some point in the future? If you buy a home and you need to sell at some point down the road, do you know if you are going to make money or take a loss? Probably not. Most investments have a "significant downside penalty" that you usually don't know ahead of time. The annuity is one of the only investments you can make that tells you exactly what the worst-case scenario is right from the beginning. From that standpoint, it's nice to know that if you need your money out of your annuity, you can get it, and you will know how much the penalty will be.

Let's say that you have an indexed annuity, and in year five the surrender charge is 5 percent. Chances are that you'll have earned more than 5 percent over that time period. Most annuities will just take the 5 percent penalty and not the earned interest. In a good market, you could have earned 20 percent or more. That means if you want all your money at the end of five years, you're going to pay a 5 percent penalty and still wind up 15 percent ahead. When you put it in perspective, the reality is that the surrender fee is really more of a surcharge than a "significant penalty."

It may also interest you to know why insurance companies apply a penalty should you want to withdraw your money early. It is not because they want to handcuff you and needlessly imprison your money against your will. Rather, it is because they are investing in assets that correspond to the length of time that you're willing to commit your money for. In the case of a ten-year annuity, they may purchase bonds that will mature in ten years. As discussed earlier, they will get their principal back as long as they hold the bond to maturity. If you want to cash out early, they may need to sell some bonds at an unfavorable price to get you your cash. By imparting a surrender fee, they're simply transferring any losses to you because of your decision to withdraw early.

"THE FEES ARE OUTRAGEOUS."

Yes, but only with regards to variable annuities. That's one of the reasons I don't like variable annuities. Most of the articles I've read that say the fees are outrageous are talking about fixed annuities, indexed annuities, and variable annuities all at the same time. Most writers who write financial articles don't really understand the nuances between the different types of annuities. They tend to convolute the different features and drawbacks of all annuities in one article; so when they say the fees are outrageous, people tend to think that the fees of all annuities are outrageous, but that's not the case.

I believe that the fees on variable annuities are outrageous, often exceeding 3 percent and sometimes even 4 percent; many of the other annuities, even most index annuities, have no fees whatsoever. If you want to add a guaranteed lifetime income rider to your annuity, then there may be a fee for that; and even then, the fee is only around 1 percent annually, which is less than a lot of mutual fund fees—plus it is optional. If you don't need or want the guaranteed lifetime income, and you just want the annuity for safety of principal and potential for higher returns, then there is no fee from most annuity companies. If you are purchasing any annuity other than a variable annuity, then it is a myth that fees are outrageous.

The Politics Of Annuities

If you do an online search of annuities, you're often going to come up with a negative impression. The reality is that most annuities are insurance products, not investments. Over the last couple of decades, there's been a battle going on between the Securities and Exchange Commission (SEC) and the insurance departments of the various states. The SEC wants to regulate indexed annuities as securities. Their logic is that because it's tied to a stock market index, and because stock market investments are securities, then the SEC should be the regulatory agency that oversees annuities. They don't often mention that if annuities are classified as securities, the SEC gets to charge a fee to the insurance companies for offering them.

Because indexed annuities are insurance products, the SEC has no regulatory authority over them. They are losing a lot of fees that they would be collecting if they regulated them. Why is this? Because indexed annuities are relatively new. Indexed annuities have only been around since 1996. Relative to the world of stocks, which have been around for several hundred years, they are a fairly new investment. Because they allow you to participate in the stock market gains while giving you the same safety of the bank, hundreds of billions of dollars have flown out of mutual funds, which are regulated by the SEC, and into annuities, which are not. Since the SEC cannot collect fees on what it doesn't regulate, they have a financial interest in regulating annuities.

The SEC isn't the only entity that bad-mouths annuities every chance it gets. A lot of advisors involved in securities selling—the sale of stocks and mutual funds—are not enthusiastic about annuities either. Many of them will tell you that they literally hate annuities. Why? Is it because annuities are not a good investment? Is it because annuities are not capable of providing a good return on your investment? No.

Here again, it is due to plain old-fashioned greed. Annuities do not pay a continuous residual commission like mutual funds do. Fee-only advisors don't get to charge their normal annual fee on any annuities that they recommend. Therefore, they don't recommend them.

Full disclosure, I am a fee-only advisor. If you're going to put a half a million dollars into an annuity, I can't charge you an annual management fee of 1 percent on that money. I'm going to get paid a onetime commission for recommending that annuity, because it is an insurance product, not an investment. Depending on the insurance company, the commission could be anywhere from 5 to 7 percent or so.

Let's say you have $500,000 to invest. Your advisor has a choice as to how to invest your money. They can choose to get a onetime commission for selling you an annuity. Or they can choose to charge you 1 percent a year or more on that $500,000 as long as you're a client or until you die. If you had that choice, onetime commission of 6 percent or 1 percent per year of $500,000 each year for the life of the client, which would you choose?

From a purely business standpoint, it makes more sense for advisors to put you into investments that will pay them a residual 1 percent fee or more each year for the rest of your life instead of collecting a onetime commission on the annuity. If they've built their practice around the residual fee they're charging you, it makes more financial sense for them to recommend the investment that pays them residually for the rest of your life. The fact that hundreds of billions of dollars have flown out of mutual funds into annuities just adds fuel to fire.

The reason many advisors bad-mouth annuities has nothing to do with their performance. It has everything to do with that advisor's business model and their reason for being in the financial industry. The securities world of stocks and bonds dwarfs the insurance world.

It's exponentially bigger. When you watch CNBC or Fox Business, you're going to see more ads by companies selling mutual funds and securities than you are by insurance companies selling annuities. When the typical consumer walks into the front door of your office looking for investment advice, even a mediocre financial advisor can tell within minutes the level of financial knowledge and understanding of the person with whom he or she is talking. If all that advisor cares about is making money for himself, he can take someone who has been indoctrinated by the media and steer them into an investment that is going to perform okay for the investor and provide the advisor with substantial commissions and fees. He's just doing his job. I know a lot of advisors who can do that and sleep well at night. I am not one of them. I don't run with the herd. My philosophy is doing what is in the best interest of my client for the long term.

Let me give you an illustration. I have a client named Michael. He's been a client of mine since 2006. Michael is currently seventy-seven years old and is a very bright, upright, and sophisticated individual. Before he retired, he was a very successful businessman.

Michael has over $1 million in annuities.

I was talking with Michael recently.

"Anthony, with all the negative press that there is about annuities, if you were going to try to recommend an annuity to me today, I would never buy one," he said. "But the fact is that I bought a million dollars' worth of annuities from you back in 2006, and I absolutely love them. I understand how they work. My principal is protected, and I've gotten a decent rate of return all along the way. I was not affected by the major market crash of 2008, and I know that my money is protected if we have another major crash to come."

I am in this business to do what is right for people in the long run. I don't believe annuities are right for everyone, but neither are mutual funds or any other type of investment. Should everyone have life insurance? Should everyone have bonds? Should everyone own individual stock? The reality is that there is no particular investment that is right for everyone. And that's also true for annuities.

Annuities are not a good match for people who want to take risks or get in, make a quick killing on a fast-moving stock, and then get out. I tend to think that annuities are right

I am in this business to do what is right for people in the long run.

for people who are more concerned about safety and guaranteed income than they are growth.

If you are a person who is more concerned about safety than you are about growth or more concerned about protecting your principal, and you're comfortable with not getting double-digit returns, then an annuity may be what you're looking for. I know many people who have annuities and understand how they work because I've taken the time to explain how they work and why they are a great investment vehicle for them and their situation. They love them, and I've earned my commission. And don't worry about me. I sleep well at night because I know I have done what is best for my client.

CHAPTER NINE

What You Don't Know about Estate Planning

THE MAJORITY OF PEOPLE think of estate planning as the instructions rich people give for the care of their valuables after they die. That is the popular notion, but that is only a fraction of what estate planning really is. Portions of your estate plan can be initiated should you or a loved one become incapacitated and unable to make decisions on your own.

In addition to a will and trusts, some of the many things involved in an estate plan are as follows:

- An advanced medical directive—critical for everyone eighteen years of age or older under HIPAA

- A durable power of attorney for assets

- Guardianship instructions

Let's start by establishing the reasons for an estate plan. Everything you own will be passed on to someone else after you die in one of only two ways—either under probate law or contract law. As the names suggest, if you pass your estate under probate law, it will have to go through probate before it gets to your heirs. Alternatively, if your estate passes under contract law, probate may be avoided. A good estate plan will aim to allow your estate to pass under contract law and avoid probate altogether. Allow me to flesh this out so you have a better understanding of the difference.

Probate Law

Probate is a legal process where the estate is distributed according to state law or your will. Many people incorrectly believe that having a will allows your estate to avoid probate. It does not—at least in California, which is where I am admitted to practice as an attorney. If you live in a different state, check with a qualified attorney. You don't want your beneficiaries to go through the hassle and expense of probate needlessly just because you did not know the law.

The process can take up to twenty-four months or longer depending upon the complexity of the estate and the state jurisdiction. In the case of more complex estates, probate can last for decades, as is evidenced by Michael Jackson's estate. The process in some states is fairly easy, while in other states, like California, it can be fairly difficult and lengthy.

In the following table, you will see citations to estate and probate laws for all fifty states and the District of Columbia. Many states have adopted the Uniform Probate Code, which represents an all-inclusive standard meant to simplify the probate process and to encourage similarity of laws among different states. It has been adopted, in whole or in part, by about twenty states. To access this information online, use the state name and law information as your search term, such as "Alabama title 43 chapter 2 administration of estates."

Alabama	Title 43 Chapter 2 Administration of Estates Title 43 Chapter 8 Probate Code
Alaska	Title 13 Decedents' Estates, Guardianships, Transfers and Trusts Title 13 Chapter 16 Probate of Wills and Administration
Arizona	Title 14 Trusts, Estates and Protective Proceedings
Arkansas	Title 28 Wills, Estates and Fiduciary Relationships
California	California Probate Code
Colorado	Title 15 Probate, Trusts and Fiduciaries
Connecticut	Title 45 Probate Courts and Procedure
Delaware	Title 12 Decedents' Estates and Fiduciary Relations
District of Columbia	Division III Title 18 Wills Division III Title 19 Descent Distribution and Trusts Division III Title 20 Probate and Administration of Decedents' Estates
Florida	Title XLII Estates and Trusts
Georgia	Title 53 Wills, Trusts, and Administration of Estates
Hawaii	Title 30A Uniform Probate Code
Idaho	Title 15 Uniform Probate Code
Illinois	Chapter 755 Estates Chapter 760 Trusts and Fiduciaries
Indiana	Title 29 Probate Title 30 Trusts and Fiduciaries
Iowa	Title XV Chapter 633 Probate Code Title XV Chapter 634 Private Foundations and Charitable Trusts Title XV Chapter 635 Administration of Small Estates Title XV Chapter 636 Sureties-Fiduciaries-Trusts-Investments
Kansas	Chapter 59 Probate Code
Kentucky	Chapter 140 Inheritance and Estate Taxes Chapter 386 Administration of Trusts - Investments Chapter 391 Descent and Distribution Chapter 394 Wills Chapter 395 Personal Representatives Chapter 396 Claims Against Decedents' Estates
Louisiana	Book III, Title I Of Successions Uniform Probate Law
Maine	Title 18 Decedents' Estates and Fiduciary Relations Title 18A Probate Code
Maryland	Titles 1 to 16 Estates and Trusts
Massachusetts	MGL Part II, Title II Descent and Distribution, Wills, Estates
Michigan	Chapters 701 to 713 Probate Code
Minnesota	Chapters 524-532 Estates of Decedents; Guardianships
Mississippi	Title 91 Trusts and Estates

Source: FindLaw, "State Laws; Estates & Probate," https://www.findlaw.com/estate/planning-an-estate/state-laws-estates-probate.html.

TABLE J

Missouri	Title XXXI, Chapters 456-475 Trusts and Estates of Decedents
Montana	Title 72 Estates, Trusts and Fiduciary Relationships
Nebraska	Chapter 30 Decedents' Estates; Protection of Persons and Property
Nevada	Title 12 Wills and Estates of Deceased Persons Title 13 Guardianships; Conservatorships; Trusts
New Hampshire	Title LVI Probate Courts and Decedents' Estates
New Jersey	Titles 3A and 3B Administration of Estates — Decedents and Others
New Mexico	Chapter 45 Uniform Probate Code Chapter 46 Fiduciaries and Trusts
New York	Chapter 17-B Estates, Powers and Trusts
North Carolina	Chapter 41 Estates Chapter 47 Probate and Registration
North Dakota	Title 30.1 Uniform Probate Code
Ohio	Title XXI Courts - Probate - Juvenile
Oklahoma	Title 58 Probate Procedure Title 84 Wills and Succession
Oregon	Chapter 111 Probate Law Chapter 112 Intestate Succession and Wills Chapter 113 Initiation of Estate Proceedings Chapter 114 Administration of Estates Chapter 115 Claims, Actions, and Suits Against Estates
Pennsylvania	Title 20 Decedents, Estates and Fiduciaries
Rhode Island	Title 33 Probate Practice and Procedure
South Dakota	Title 29A Uniform Probate Code Title 55 Fiduciaries and Trusts
South Carolina	Title 21 Estates, Trusts, Guardians and Fiduciaries Title 62 Probate Code
Tennessee	Title 30 Administration of Estates Title 31 Descent and Distribution Title 32 Wills Title 35 Fiduciaries and Trust Estates
Texas	Texas Probate Code
Utah	Title 22 Fiduciaries and Trusts Title 75 Uniform Probate Code
Vermont	Title 14 Decedents' Estates and Fiduciary Relations
Virginia	Title 64.2 Wills and Decedents' Estates
Washington	Title 11 Probate and Trust Law
West Virginia	Chapter 41 Wills Chapter 42 Descent and Distribution Chapter 44 Administration of Estates and Trusts
Wisconsin	Chapter 701 Trusts Chapter 853 Wills Chapters 851 to 882 Probate
Wyoming	Title 2 Wills, Decedents' Estates and Probate Code Title 2 Chapter 2 Probate Court Title 2 Chapter 6 Wills Title 2 Chapter 7 Administration of Estates

TABLE J CONTINUED

Last Will And Testament

There are multiple ways to create a last will and testament. The most common ways are to handwrite it or type it out. Either way, failure to follow the rules will impact how your estate gets distributed.

If you have not drafted a will before you die, the state intestacy laws will dictate who is entitled to your estate and how it will be distributed. If you have taken the time to draft your will, so long as it meets all of the requisite formalities, and as long as the court admits it, then the remainder of your estate will likely pass according to your will.

Outside of having to go through the probate process, there are a couple of other disadvantages of using a last will and testament to pass your estate to your heirs. One reason is that almost anyone can contest your will for any reason, valid or not. Another reason is that wills must be admitted to the court upon your demise. As a result, it becomes a public document, which allows anyone to find out the net worth of your estate and whom you owed money to upon your passing. This is how we know that when Michael Jackson died, he had $400 million of debt. Don't feel too bad for his heirs, though, because his estate has earned over $2 billion since his demise.

The will names an executor, who has a responsibility to coordinate the process with the court and carry out the will's instructions after the probate process has been completed. If there is no executor, the probate court will appoint one. The executor inventories the estate of the deceased, pays off all the decedent's debts, and pays any outstanding taxes, including federal estate tax and applicable state inheritance taxes. The executor then distributes the remaining assets as directed in the will.

Another reason to avoid probate is because it can be a very lengthy and expensive process. That's the last thing you want your loved ones to deal with at a time when they are grieving over your loss.

Contract Law

Assets that are titled as joint tenancy with rights of survivorship will transfer immediately to the surviving owner. Retirement plans, IRAs, and certain types of financial accounts allow you to name a beneficiary, and the proceeds will be paid directly to that named beneficiary upon your death. Furthermore, assets that have been placed in a trust will avoid probate as well, which is why trusts have become such a popular estate planning tool in recent times. These are all examples of assets that will pass under contract law.

How Not To Avoid Probate

There are ways to avoid probate by passing your estate under contract law even without the use of a trust. However, there are often major drawbacks to using some of these methods. For example, one way to avoid probate is through titling your accounts as joint tenancy with rights of survivorship. We see this with couples who want to make sure their family home passes to their children upon their death. They will put their kids on the title so the house will pass directly to the surviving joint tenants, the kids, while they are still living. The drawback to this is that legally, the kids now own half the property. Once you make them owners, they have to sign off if you don't want them to own it anymore. That can be a big problem if relationships go south somewhere down the road.

We had a situation where a couple put their two sons on the title to the family home. The sons were model students and athletes at their high school, were active in the community, and were growing into very responsible young men. During the older son's junior year of college, the brothers formed a band. Four years later, the father pulled the plug on paying college tuition for the twentysomethings, who rarely went to class. The band was becoming popular and had graduated from college town bars to regional opening acts for touring bands. They had a hit song and made a little money, so they moved back home and built a studio and rehearsal space off the back of the garage.

Now the parents had their adult children back home with them. Their nice early American ranch on the estate-sized lot was no longer the refuge of successful professionals who were enjoying the autumn of their careers. It was more like a frat house. The band and crew members were mostly nice and respectable young men who confined themselves to the kitchen, family room, and basement. The recording engineer and the bass player were "renting" the pool house. There were cars, trucks, and a converted Greyhound bus parked on or next to the driveway.

The parents smiled bravely and adjusted to those changes. It was even interesting and kind of exciting at first, until their house became infiltrated by the band's followers. There were the girlfriends and a blend of different friends—then came the abundance of alcohol, the appearance of drugs, the partying, the music, and the drama.

It came to a head one night when the parents called the police after a fight broke out and windows were shattered. The officers came over and asked who owned the house, with the intention of telling all the guests to leave. But when they discovered the sons were legal owners, their hands were somewhat tied. Apparently, if the owner wants his guests to stay, there's not much the police can do but give a stern warning. It was a standoff between the parents and the sons.

As bad as that situation became, it could have been worse. The sons could have gotten into serious trouble or failed to pay their taxes and had a lien put against the property. All this anxiety could have been avoided if the parents had just transferred the house into a revocable living trust, which would have helped the owners avoid this situation entirely for reasons that we will discuss next.

A revocable trust would have accomplished their noble-sounding end goal, but they would have had the leverage to resist having their adult children move back in with them in the first place. They avoided probate, but they still ended up in court when they sued to have their sons removed from the title.

Trust Basics

As we mentioned, trusts are used to protect assets, minimize taxes, and avoid probate. There are many different types of trust entities that can be structured to accomplish different purposes. These include revocable, irrevocable, living, testamentary, asset protection, charitable, special needs, spendthrift, and more. As we witnessed in the case of the band parents, a revocable trust would have been beneficial in their situation, because it can be changed over time. An irrevocable trust means the operational characteristics of the trust cannot be changed. A living trust is one created while the grantor is alive, whereas a testamentary trust is created by the will of the grantor. An asset protection trust protects the grantor's assets from creditors. A charitable trust is an irrevocable trust designed to use the assets of the trust for the benefit of a charitable organization. A special-needs trust allows a disabled or chronically ill person to receive income without reducing their eligibility for public assistance benefits. A spendthrift trust protects the assets or corpus of the trust from a beneficiary who may be financially irresponsible.

Trusts are a common estate planning tool because they can lower or eliminate estate taxes, significantly reduce or even eliminate capital gains tax on the sale of appreciated assets, create a charitable tax deduction, and avoid probate.

Because the most common type of trust today is the revocable living trust, the rest of our discussion will revolve around this.

REVOCABLE LIVING TRUST

While it is true that an individual can set up a trust without an attorney, I almost never recommend that. Having an attorney to translate the legal terminology and guide you through the process will save you time, money, and stress in the long run.

When you set up a revocable trust, you are establishing a contract with your beneficiaries that you can change at any point in time for any reason.

If there are minor children involved, the trust can specify how they will be provided for and when or if they will gain control of the estate's finances.

For example, the trustee can approve that your nineteen-year-old son purchase a car to go to college, but the trust isn't going to pay for a Maserati when a Mazda-rati will do just fine. The trust gives the trustee the authority and the discretion to act in the best interest of the beneficiary and to preserve the corpus of the trust. Your choice of a successor trustee is not something you want to take lightly. It should be someone who can figuratively step into your shoes in every financial situation; and a good estate planner can help you by walking you through all your options.

What happens to you if you have a stroke and suddenly cannot make your own decisions? A revocable trust will allow your trustees to take over in the event you become incapacitated before you pass away. When you have all your required documents in place, you'll find that estate planning allows for a peaceful and confident state of mind.

In addition to establishing the trust, you must also fund it. Right now, you own your checking account, your home, and your assets. Once you're done setting up a trust, you transfer your accounts to the trust, and your trust owns everything—but you control the trust. You own nothing, but you control everything. This is the reason why having a trust avoids probate. Because when you pass away, only the creator of the trust died; the trust itself didn't die, which is why they call it a living trust.

One of the biggest mistakes I have seen made in estate planning deals with assumptions. Because people don't know, they assume that once they have created the trust and signed the papers, their assets are automatically put into the trust. It doesn't work that way. Starting with your checking and savings accounts, everything must be changed over from your name to the name of the trust. Although this may sound difficult, it is actually very easy.

Michael Jackson's estate was still in probate more than a decade after he passed away. Jackson had actually done some estate planning, and all the attorneys indicated that his trust was well drafted and would have done exactly what he wanted it to do except for one not-so-minor mistake. He never funded it. And not funding a trust is equivalent to not having a trust at all, which is why his estate had to pass under probate law instead of passing under contract law.

Properties and land have to be transferred into the trust by transferring the title to the property in your name as trustee. When I established the Saccaro Living Trust, of which my wife and I are the trustees, I wrote up a new deed and transferred the property to "Anthony and Anca Saccaro, trustees of the Saccaro Living Trust" with a signature and date of execution.

Transfer of all other personal property that does not have a title, deed, or certificate of ownership will be done through a general assignment. With one signature, this document assigns all your personal belongings to the trust. Items like your furniture, electronics, artwork, jewelry, sporting goods, vehicles, recreational equipment, clothing, and all the stuff in your garage. Fortunately for you, this means you do not have to put Post-it Notes on every piece of property you own.

The trust survives you, dictating what happens after you die. Do you want to give everything to everyone at once? Do you want to spread distributions out over time? Do you want to give to charities? These decisions are all made when you establish the trust, and it's all handled by the person you have named as the trustee.

Importantly, not everything you own can or should be transferred into your trust. Investment and retirement accounts such as annuities, 401(k) plans, 403(b) plans, and IRAs have named beneficiaries and generally do not need to be transferred into the trust, because they already pass under contract law. Most assets that generally pass under contract law already avoid probate, so there may not be a need to title them into the trust.

Additionally, it is important to recognize that your nontrust assets need to be coordinated with your trust assets to make sure that your property is distributed according to your wishes. Some people want to give a percentage to charity, so they name the charity in their trust for a certain percentage, believing that the percentage will be calculated based on their entire estate; however, that percentage is going to be based only on the value of the trust assets and not on assets that are held outside of a trust, such as life insurance and retirement accounts.

You don't have to be rich to have a trust or an estate plan. If you fail to plan, the state and federal governments and attorneys will be happy to handle your estate for you, and they will charge a hefty price for doing so.

In addition to a trust or will, you need a pour-over will, powers of attorney, advanced medical directive, and other documents that will ensure your wishes are carried out at those times when you are unable to make your wishes known.

Pour-Over Will

Many people think that once they have set up a trust, they no longer need a will. This would be true in a perfect world. If all your assets have been transferred into your trust as they should have been, then you really don't need a will. What often happens, though, is that you either forget to transfer the deed to the fishing cabin or, more likely, you just go on living and acquire more assets without ever titling them in the trust. I've seen people open a new financial account and forget to put it in the name of the trust.

To avoid that, we use a will that is specifically drafted to work with the trust. It's called a "pour-over" will. As long as the assets you leave outside the trust do not meet the qualifications for probate, they will be allowed to transfer (pour over) into the trust and be treated as if they had been retitled from inception.

Advanced Healthcare Directive

President Bill Clinton signed the Health Insurance Portability and Accountability Act (HIPAA) into law on August 21, 1996,[28] and it's been periodically updated ever since. The goals of HIPAA are to protect health insurance coverage for workers and their families when they change or lose their jobs (portability) and to protect health data integrity, confidentiality, and availability (accountability).

This law has made it illegal for doctors to give medically identifiable information about you to anyone, including your spouse and adult children, without your consent.

---

28 govinfo, "Anniversary of HIPAA," https://www.govinfo.gov/features/
HIPAA#:~:text=As%20recorded%20in%20Book%202,be%20measured%2C%20
peace%20of%20mind.

Prior to HIPAA, the laws allowed you to dictate which people could give information to the doctors, but the doctors were free to give information to whoever requested it. Under the current version of HIPAA, without a properly executed advance healthcare directive (AHD), medical personnel cannot legally give out your information without your expressed consent.

An AHD not only allows doctors to inform the directed family members about your condition, it also allows those family members to give feedback to the doctors regarding your care.

A properly drafted AHD allows the person to whom you have given authority to make medical decisions on your behalf, making sure your wishes are followed after you are no longer able to make decisions for yourself. The AHD can be changed alongside your life conditions and desires, and it should include a "living will." A living will tells medical professionals which procedures they may or may not perform in order to save or prolong your life.

Some other advance care planning documents that might be needed at the end of life include a do-not-resuscitate (DNR) order and an organ and tissue donation directive.

Guardianship Directives

Besides the AHD, there are other documents that should be in your estate plan. If you have minor children or are the legal guardian of minor children, you need to have a guardianship directive (GD). A GD appoints someone to speak on behalf of others who cannot speak for themselves either because they are minors or because they have suffered through some sort of incapacitating event.

Do you know who would take care of your children if you and your spouse died suddenly? Most people think that their children would automatically go to their closest relatives, but that is not necessarily what happens.

In 1997, the Uniform Child Custody Jurisdiction and Enforcement Act (UCCJEA) was drafted by the National Conference of Commissioners on Uniform State Laws. The law recognizes that a minor child is not property and cannot simply be bequeathed to someone in the event of the parents' deaths. A judge, usually in the family court, surrogate court, or district court, will have the final say over what happens to minor children in the event of the custodial parent's death or removal; however, they give considerable weight to the opinion of that parent if there is a pertinent, well-thought-out directive to which the judge can refer.

In your guardianship directive, you can designate one person to be both the guardian of the person and the guardian of the estate. This is often a good idea if you have another family member who has agreed to raise your children as their own; however, there are some things you need to consider when selecting that person. First, are they fit for the role? He or she will be responsible for ensuring your child's physical, emotional, and spiritual well-being. Beyond providing food, shelter, clothing, and healthcare for your child, they will also be responsible for the quality of your child's education and intellectual growth, their values, their lifestyle choices, and their religious beliefs. Does the chosen guardian share your beliefs and your core values? Do they have the resources needed to raise your child as you would? Are they the type of person who is going to give your child the necessary time, energy, and emotional commitment needed to raise a healthy and happy child into a responsible, successful adult?

If your estate is sizable, you can appoint one person as guardian of the person and another as guardian of the estate. The primary reason for doing this is to make sure the person who has agreed to raise your child is acting in your child's best interest and not with a financial motive. The guardian of the estate has the responsibility to manage the assets until the estate can be legally transferred to your adult child. The guardian of the estate can be directed to pay any and all costs incurred by the guardian of the person directly related to raising your child, or it can be set up as a monthly allotment. Either way, it may be a good idea to appoint two different people in those capacities.

Durable Power Of Attorney

Another important legal document is the durable power of attorney for asset management. The "durable" part means that the document stays in effect should you become incapacitated and unable to handle matters on your own. When you set up a trust and put all your assets in the trust, you choose successor trustees to administer the trust after you are gone. The successor trustees have the authority to act on your behalf with regard to the assets that are in the trust. But what about your retirement accounts, annuities, or any other assets that are outside of the trust? The successor trustees have no authority over any of that, because those accounts are not in the trust.

The durable power of attorney gives the people you choose the ability to make decisions and act as if they were you with regard to accounts that are not in the trust. Most people choose the successor trustees to simultaneously act as their agents under their durable power of attorney. That way, they can properly handle all assets that are both inside and outside the trust should you become incapacitated.

Estate Planning Plans Your Life

Estate planning helps you navigate through your financial growth years with clarity and peace of mind. Your property ownership is protected and transferred in a smooth and orderly process at the appropriate time. Your tax liabilities are minimized and managed through the use of an experienced advisor.

> *Estate planning helps you navigate through your financial growth years with clarity and peace of mind.*

Some have said that estate planning has given them a renewed sense of gratitude for what they have accomplished and all the blessings they have received. I know that going through my father's passing caused me to take stock of my life and see the importance of protecting my legacy for my wife and my children. My faith and my preparation have eliminated the fear of dying and allowed me to fully appreciate and enjoy every day that God has given me.

On a much more personal note, if you are afraid of dying, I urge you to make peace with Jesus Christ, as I have, and get that relationship in order. If you don't know how and would like a simple guide that explains the peace and happiness that comes with eternal estate planning, contact me and I will be happy to send you a free book that will explain how you can be pardoned from your sin through Christ's work on the cross. While setting up your earthly estate plan is important, it is even more important to have your eternal estate plan set up. Life on this Earth is like a vapor that vanishes as quickly as it was breathed out. But eternity is forever. I implore you to make sure you know where you are going to spend your eternity.

CHAPTER TEN

What Women Should Know about Investing

A Woman Speaks About Investing

A book written to help you discover what you don't know about retirement would not be complete if I did not bring up the differences between men and women when it comes to investing.

Men tend to be performance-based investors and often treat the accumulation of money as if it were a contact sport. They want to watch their account balance get bigger each month, even if it requires them to take risks that they can't afford to take. Forget the fact that they've already won the game by having accumulated enough dollars to last them the rest of their lives; they want their money to keep performing because investing is a game and they're competitive. If their money stops growing, they feel as if they're losing. And they don't want to lose. I refer to this as "performance-based investing."

For women, on the other hand, the purpose of their money is to provide security and peace of mind. They don't care how their portfolio performs, as long as it is invested so as to accomplish their purpose. If they have accumulated enough points to win the game of life, they are very happy to shift their focus from taking risks to protecting their principal, because it allows them to sleep well. I refer to this as "purpose-based investing."

I believe that purpose-based investing is the more common-sense approach. Once your investments have accomplished their purpose, it makes sense to reevaluate your position to decide whether you need to make a change. If you sit down at a Las Vegas slot machine with the purpose of winning two hundred bucks to pay for the cost of your room for the night, then once you've won those two hundred dollars (if ever), you've accomplished your goal. If you are a purpose-based investor, you will get up and walk away knowing you've accomplished what you set out to do. If you are a performance-based investor, even though you've already won, you will continue to stay at the slot machine and needlessly risk losing your gains.

As you are in the throes of the accumulation phase of life, the purpose of your investment strategy is to grow your portfolio as large as possible so that when you get to retirement, your investments can provide you with income. If you get to retirement and your nest egg is sizable enough to provide the income you need for the rest of your life, congratulations, you've accomplished your purpose. You've won the game of life. Now what? That depends if you're a performance-based investor or a purpose-based investor.

If you're a performance-based investor, you'll continue playing offense and taking unnecessary risks with your investments even though you've already accomplished what you intended to. If you're a purpose-based investor, because you've already accomplished your goal, you'll take a more defensive stance. You'll conclude that while your previous purpose was to accumulate as much as possible with a focus on growth, your new purpose is to protect your portfolio with a focus on income. Because your purpose has changed, you'll adjust your investment strategy accordingly.

Because women tend to be more purpose-based than men, and because women and men treat their money and retirement differently, I thought it may be best to let a woman discuss those differences through her eyes. So, I asked Lorraine A. Grossman to write this chapter. Lorraine is an excellent advisor with years of experience, and there are not too many people who I trust more than her. If I was looking for someone to advise me about my retirement and investment strategies, I would turn to Lorraine in a heartbeat. There is no one who works harder at being excellent in her profession than she does, and she has the heart of a teacher. That being said, here is Lorraine's point of view on the difference between men and women when it comes to investing.

LORRAINE'S POINT OF VIEW

Before joining Anthony Saccaro and the rest of the Providence Financial team in 2014, I spent more than sixteen years working at Pepperdine University School of Law.

Many women are making an impact in the world of finance. One of those women is Sallie Krawcheck, the CEO and cofounder of Ellevest, a digital financial advisor for women.[29] Named by *Forbes* magazine as one of the most powerful women in finance, Krawcheck was the first person to introduce me to the concept of irrational exuberance. This concept was described by former Wall Street trader John Coates when his observations revealed that there is a different mindset between men and women when it comes to investing. He suggested that testosterone

---

29 *Forbes*, "Sallie Krawcheck," https://www.forbes.com/profile/
   sallie-krawcheck/?sh=6471c72a137a.

caused men to take increased risks.[30] Under its influence, they were lulled into a feeling of invincibility. When the market turned downward, testosterone was replaced by rising cortisol levels, causing men to rush from fight to flight. The study showed this hormonal switch led to diminished decision-making capabilities, which exacerbated the problem. Women, on the other hand, were more prudent. They took fewer risks, avoided losses, and ended up with higher earnings over the same period.

Krawcheck's takeaway from the Coates study mirrors the approach I use in my job every day. I tell women to take the time to plan carefully. Buy low and sell when you have reached your goal. The many differences between the way women and men invest is why I am so excited to share my expertise to urge and educate women on how to plan without a man and take responsibility for their financial future by learning how to invest wisely now.

The Female Philosophy Of Investing

There have been many different polls and statistics about the difference in how men and women invest. They all seem to come to the same conclusion that men tend to be more aggressive and take more chances, whereas women tend to be more reserved and cautious. The differences may be due to how we've been raised or that men and women think and process things differently. I think another reason women tend to be little bit more conservative is because historically women have been focused on family and what they can do to make a dollar stretch to make ends meet.

Here in California, we are always planning for an earthquake. We never want it to happen, but we prepare for it. The scientific data

---

30   *Forbes*, "Neuroscience Explains Why Wall Street Needs More Women,"
     December 21, 2012, https://www.forbes.com/sites/karlmoore/2012/12/21/
     neuroscience-explains-why-wall-street-needs-more-women/?sh=1c44de7e428b.

tells us that it is more probable than not that one will happen in the near future. We also prepare for wildfires and plan our escape routes, because the historical data tells us that there is a high probability that there is going to be a wildfire somewhere nearby. Women need to adopt this defensive posture when thinking about their finances.

Women And Financial Planning

Women work hard to make their money, but they're not investing it properly. Some are not investing at all, or if they do invest, they are not staying on top of it.

Many times, women I meet with just take the information I give them at face value. While I am flattered to have earned that level of trust, I would rather you take the time to get a second opinion. I run into that a lot—where women will candidly admit that they just assumed that it was so. That is how you get into trouble.

Tell me that you want to do a little research before you jump in with both feet; then do it. Sometimes women are a little bit too trusting. You need to make sure that you don't get involved in something that is not good. People say, "If it sounds too good to be true, then it probably is."

Some Things Women Think About Money

I recently reached out to a friend of mine to discuss her thoughts on women and investing. Rachel and I came to know each other through our children. Her son and my daughter went through high school together about twelve years ago. She had recently attended one of my Social Security seminars in California. We had not been in touch since our kids graduated from high school, but I immediately recognized her and could tell she didn't recognize me. She scheduled a meeting with me to discuss when would be the best time for her to file for Social Security. As we started the meeting, I could see she still did not recognize me, so I asked her if she remembered who I was. She didn't. When I reminded her that my daughter and her son went to Oak Park High School together, the pieces came together. She remarked how much I had changed, and we rekindled our friendship.

Through the course of our meeting, Rachel admitted that she really didn't have a good grasp on what she was invested in. She had left the investing up to her advisor—mainly because she was so busy working. Now she was trying to become more knowledgeable about her portfolio, because she had recently changed her career. Her new career made a tremendous change in her income, and her quality of life had improved immensely. She wanted to know how to protect her portfolio and keep it growing.

When our meeting came to a close, Rachel admitted that she had never heard about the importance of making a paradigm shift from investing for accumulation to investing for distribution as you approach retirement. Because this was such a revelation to her, she wanted me to educate some of her friends about the strategies I taught her. What had really opened her eyes was the analogy I used to describe the difference between the two strategies.

"The primary reason you buy a rental home," I shared, "is to produce consistent income from rent that you can live off of. The value of the home is going to fluctuate over time, but as long as the rent shows up each month, how much does the fluctuation affect you?"

"Not at all," she correctly replied.

"Well, that's how investing for income works. When you invest in a portfolio designed to give you income, your portfolio is going to fluctuate. Regardless of the fluctuation, though, the investments will provide a consistent stream of rent that you can live off, without ever touching your principal; we just call the rent interest and dividends."

"I wish I had known this concept twenty years ago when I was making a good living," Rachel said. "I would have taken charge of my own investing, and I'm sure I would have been in a much better position now. There are a lot of women out there who need to hear what you have to say."

She invited me to an open house she was having for her new business. When I arrived, she introduced me to several women who were attending. As she was introducing me, she shared how I educated her on the difference between investing for growth and investing for income.

I was grateful for her generous introduction and have thanked her, because it really got me thinking about women and investing. There is a real need to bring women up to speed on their knowledge of investing and teach them what they are missing out on.

Rachel's story is not unique, so when I reached out to her regarding her thoughts about women and investing, she began to share with me some insights of the women I had met at her open house and their views on finances. They were from all different walks of life, but each one had a story that illustrated the need for them to get help. Each woman there represents hundreds of women with the same or similar stories. The following are stories you may relate to, coupled with my insight on what they may not have considered regarding their finances. The names have been changed to protect their privacy.

Stories Women Have Shared With Me

Cheryl is a very smart woman with an MBA and an executive position with an insurance company. She is very proud that she isn't like the majority of women who have their husband handle the finances because they really don't understand the investing world.

She understands investing fairly well but has made it known that her husband handles the investments solely because he is an accountant and is better at numbers than she is, not because she doesn't understand them. Her expertise is in IT and data management.

In this situation, Cheryl and her husband have an understanding that works well for them. But there was a blind spot in her retirement plan that is common to a lot of married women.

"What will happen to you if your husband suddenly passes away?" I asked.

Too many women never let themselves consider life without their partner, but it is a statistical probability that needs to be planned for. In Cheryl's case, I would encourage her to have their financial advisor go over everything they have in their portfolio and come up with a plan that addresses this.

> *Too many women never let themselves consider life without their partner, but it is a statistical probability that needs to be planned for.*

"Make sure your advisor explains every aspect of your retirement plan and what it is designed for," I would tell her. "Have him or her go over the pros and cons with both of you so you can identify any oversights in your planning. You must understand why you are invested the way you are. That way if something should happen to your husband, you are not thrown into handling the finances with no knowledge of your investments or whether you have enough income to carry you through retirement. In a time of distress, you don't want to find yourself in the position of having to trust others, hoping they have your best interests at heart."

Martina is a retired pharmaceutical representative who had a very good career and earned a nice pension from her company. She is nervous about going out with friends and is always frugal with her money. The reason for her fear is because if she spends all her money now, it won't be there later, when she needs it.

Like many retirees, Martina is a classic example of someone who is unsure if they will outlive their money. It is likely that she lacks a long-term plan and does not understand what she can and cannot do with her portfolio. Her fear of running out of money is taking the joy out of her well-earned retirement. Retirement can be miserable if you have a lot of money but are afraid to spend it. No one had ever educated her on how spending habits change when we reach retirement. She has already made major purchases, like a house, and she is long past the expense of raising children. She may want to consider selling the house and downsizing.

Women need to understand and get educated about investment and retirement strategies. They need to be aware of the cycles of money and how to put it to work for them. This is exactly what I strive to provide for women: education about how to start looking at money differently.

Rachel believes that most of her friends could benefit from financial education. I think that's probably true for most women today.

As we continued our conversation, I realized that I needed to find ways to get all women on the same playing field when it comes to increasing their knowledge about investment and financial planning. I explained that I want to create a platform where women can learn and share without becoming overwhelmed by it all.

Rachel thought it was a great idea and said, "I don't know anything about finances, and most women like myself don't know how to go about getting the information. We don't even know where to start. There are so many different books out there and videos, and it is all so confusing. In the end, it all boils down to whom you trust."

I am starting to realize that women may not grasp how much they know or do not know about investing. Many know the basics but lack the confidence to believe in what they know. When a woman becomes more confident in the world of finance, she realizes that this world is not something to avoid or approach with caution. Instead, it is something for her to embrace with excitement, knowing that it can help her gain

In my humble opinion, women and the finance world are a perfect complement to each other.

financial freedom if approached with knowledge and common sense. In my humble opinion, women and the finance world are a perfect complement to each other. I'm looking forward to seeing more and more women adding the power of financial knowledge and investing to their arsenal of financial resources.

The Nurse's Tale

I recently had a female nurse come in to see me. She was approaching retirement and was fearful that she was going to run out of money before her life was over. She said she was losing sleep and didn't know what decisions to make. She had been with another firm, and they had put all of her money into several different annuities. Now she was not sure whether that had been a good decision.

She told me her story while I sorted through the documents she had laid upon my desk. She had worked hard all her life. Her father had taught her to live within her means and save all that she could. As a result, she had worked hard and lived a frugal life, and in spite of her concerns, she seemed to have done all right for herself. Her investments had done very well, she had close to zero debt, and her home was paid off. I shared that even though she felt she did not know anything about finances and investing, she instinctively made good choices using her intelligence and common sense.

"What you are lacking is confidence," I told her. "You need to take ownership of your money and start asking questions of your advisor."

She said she tried, but he was a young man and spoke so fast that she could not understand what he was saying. She had gotten to the point where she just stopped asking. This is a dangerous situation too many women find themselves in today.

I assured her that we would never do that in my office and empowered her to always ask questions and to keep asking until she completely understood the concepts I was explaining.

"Remember," I reminded her. "This is your money, not your advisor's."

I share these examples of women and their finances because their stories and circumstances are very common. I'm finding that the more women I meet with, the more there seems to be a resounding theme. Although they are well-educated and smart women, they seem to lack confidence when it comes to their own finances and investing. This does not make sense to me, because most women are constantly budgeting for themselves and their family, making a dollar stretch further than economically possible. Maybe that in itself is the problem; they are so focused on the day-to-day living needs for themselves and their loved ones that they simply don't have time to focus on their own portfolio.

For most people, when they were children and the subject of math came up, many would sit in the back of the class hoping the teacher would not pick on them. For me, I loved it. I ran toward it. Math scares a lot of people, causing them to avoid it. The majority of people see finance as a form of math. If someone else can take care of their finances, and they don't have to deal with that "math," they are perfectly content to hand that responsibility off.

Women need to start empowering themselves and recognize that they have a voice. If you don't understand a concept, you need to speak up.

Here is a good example of how empowering a woman with financial knowledge and helping her take responsibility of her financial affairs can make a difference. A very smart and accomplished woman and her husband came to see me. She had come into some money, and her husband insisted that she meet with me, because he wanted her to make her own decisions about her money. In fact, the meeting started with him saying that he did not want to be included in the discussion but wanted me to focus on her. He shared with me that he does his own online investing and is very aggressive. He loved playing the market and the stocks to the point where he was taking some money earmarked for his retirement accounts and putting it into the stock market.

His wife, on the other hand, was ultraconservative and did not want to take the aggressive risks that he was. He encouraged her to come see me and make her own decisions. During the meeting I went through the different investment strategies and options. I illustrated how she could be conservative and still grow her portfolio through interest and dividends. I explained the difference between investing for growth and investing for income; but every time I would ask her a question, she would look at her husband for an answer, and he would always direct her back to me.

"She needs to do this on her own," he would say with sincere love in his voice.

At the end of our meeting, she decided to move forward as a client and made some concrete decisions. Due to her husband's willingness to help, I took the opportunity to empower her with more knowledge about investing. And by empowering her, I was also empowering him to help her.

"There is one thing you have to do before we meet again," I told her. "I want you to take a little money, no more than $500, and sit down with your husband each night. Learn what he does and get involved with his process by investing that $500 in your own investments."

I explained that there were two reasons that it would be good for her to do this. One is that she already knew he had put a substantial amount of money into this process. As his spouse, she needed to be comfortable with how he was investing their nest egg. If something happened to him, she needed to be able to step in and take over. The second reason is that it would become a good knowledge base for her.

"But the awesome by-product," I told her, "is that it gives you a chance to communicate with your husband about finances, stocks, and investing. It allows you to not only share in what he loves but to understand it as well."

I could tell that he wanted to share it with her, but he knew she was scared and didn't want to lose any money. I also recognized that she was trying to be the voice of balance, making sure that he wasn't doing anything that would jeopardize the family finances.

"But how are you going to create that balance," I asked her, "if you don't know anything about it?"

At our next meeting, she shared that she had done what I asked, and though the swings of the market were uncomfortable for her, she was so thankful. She now had a better understanding of the stock market and was learning something new every day. I looked over at her husband, and his smile truly lit up the room. He said it was so nice to have her see and learn what he enjoyed so much. I could physically see a difference in my client. She walked and talked with confidence—to the point that I asked if learning about finances and taking responsibility for her money made a difference in how she felt.

"Absolutely," she said, smiling. "It has made a huge difference on every level of our lives."

I've had several meetings with women whose husbands have passed away; many of them have come in with bags full of financial statements and various policies and said, "Please help me to understand this."

I met with a woman the other day whose husband passed away twelve years ago, and she informed me that he had handled all the investing. It wasn't that she couldn't handle it, but when they got married, they shared household responsibilities. His responsibility was the investing and hers was paying the bills.

Upon his passing, she became heavily reliant on her husband's advisor to make the decisions about her portfolio. She was thrown into this situation and was beholden to his advisor, since she lacked the knowledge to handle it herself. The advisor told her not to worry and that he would take care of her. She let him continue handling the accounts.

Recently she informed him that upon retirement, she wanted to take a couple thousand dollars out each month. His response was that she needed to cut down on her spending. After reviewing her portfolio, I agreed ... but only if she did not make a shift in her strategy. She was invested for growth and would have to sell shares each month to get her income. As a result, she would have been cannibalizing her portfolio every month she withdrew the funds she needed. If she wasn't willing to make a fundamental change in her investment strategy, there could be a real possibility of her running out of money in her later years. If the market made a major correction, she would run through her funds even sooner.

I explained that stocks and mutual funds are not the only game in town. If she was willing to make a paradigm shift from investing for growth to investing for income, she would generate enough interest and dividends from her portfolio to provide the income she needed each month without having to sell shares. I encouraged her to educate herself further and not to just take my word for it. I gave her a book, *The Return on Principle* by David J. Scranton, which describes how income-producing investments allow people to protect their principal while getting the income they want from their portfolio.

She confided that she had become so heavily reliant on her husband's advisor and felt he had done well for her. She just had never wanted to take the time to learn about investing and, as a result, would simply do whatever her advisor said. She was willing to cut back on her expenses and not do as much in retirement if that was what it took.

She became excited when I explained that if she simply took a little time to educate herself about investing for income, she would clearly realize that there were other options available to her that would allow her to enjoy her retirement without compressing her lifestyle. She wouldn't have to cut back on those things that she was so looking forward to doing during her golden years.

Her situation is all too common, and it's disheartening to me as an advisor. As Anthony discussed earlier in this book, most advisors specialize in investments oriented for growth. If someone desires to begin living off their investments, the only advice a growth-oriented advisor can give is to sell shares periodically to get their income. Very few advisors specialize in income-producing strategies like we do. Instead of instructing their clients to find an advisor who does, they simply tell their clients that they're going to have to cut back on their lifestyle, as happened to my client. If you don't know otherwise, you'll be forced to listen. Or run the risk of outliving your principal.

That's why I continuously tell my clients that knowledge is financial freedom. Sometimes a client will ask, "Can you just take care of all of my finances and give me a plan?" My response is always, "No, you need to take control of your money." It is your money; you earned it, and now you need to understand how it is working for you.

A Basic Investing Philosophy

I don't want to give the impression that all women are clueless when it comes to investing and finance. Something like 40 percent of investors right now are women. I met with a woman the other day, and she had really done well for herself. She was a little over fifty and had handled all her own investing for as far back as she could remember and was very successful.

"How did you choose your investments?" I inquired.

"Well. I just picked those investments that I liked or were familiar to me, like Apple and Netflix. Once something I liked caught my attention, I would do some basic research to make sure the company was solid. If it seemed to be, I bought some shares in it."

When she was younger, she had no clue what she was doing. She read everything she could get her hands on and started to feel that she was becoming more proficient as time marched on.

I asked her why she came to see me. She said at this point in her life, she was working a few jobs and just didn't have time to stay on top of it. She needed someone to take care of her now, because she recognized that there was a lot of volatility in the market and felt there was a real chance that there may be another major correction soon. She was honest enough with herself to admit that she truly didn't know what to do in this phase of life.

She is a perfect example of a woman who has taken the time to educate herself so she can take control of her finances. It is also a good example of the power that women have when it comes to investing.

My parting words to you—be true to yourself and recognize that you are in charge of your financial well-being and economic freedom. This starts with communicating with others, including financial professionals, asking questions, and planning for the "what ifs" that life may send your way. Come up with a solid financial game plan that works for you and allows you to maintain a good quality of life now and in the future. I believe in you.

CHAPTER ELEVEN

In Their Own Words

WE ARE BOMBARDED by advertisements from financial sales-people on a daily basis, and the underlying message is pretty consistent across the board. "You have to be in the stock market; you have to invest in mutual funds; you aren't smart enough to do it without our help, because we know our way through the pitfalls of the financial jungle."

These dishonest messages are becoming more predictable, which is why many people don't trust Wall Street. All they see are sales-people selling financial snake oil, rich people getting richer, and the rest of us getting left further and further behind. No wonder there is such a growing call for fundamental change in our economic system. This is not the first time in the history of our nation that we have tackled the issue of economic injustice, but history has shown that the answer seldom lies with government remedies. More often than not, the solution out of Washington, DC, just creates temporary stop-gap solutions and ends up creating other problems.

My mission is to educate people about a better way. It requires gaining knowledge and taking personal responsibility, but it works.

There is a time for growth investing, but there comes a time when you need to start planning for your retirement, and that requires understanding and switching over to income investing.

The Perspective of My Peers

Gregory Melia, with Melia Wealth Advisory, has been a financial advisor in Tulsa, Oklahoma, for thirty-one years. He is also a fellow member of Advisors' Academy and has known me for the last dozen years. He was asked about me by an interviewer who was writing about some of the advisors that David Scranton has gathered together under the Advisors' Academy banner. David Scranton has taught Greg and me an educational approach to investing.

Here is what Greg had to say about me:

"The first time Anthony and I met, I realized fairly quickly that our values are very much the same. Anthony's always going to do what's best for those around him first. That's a very consistent thing about him, and he carries that into his practice for his clients. That's two ways that he and I are very similar, and we've always had a connection because of it. He is also extremely trustworthy. You can confide in him and trust him with your honest, deepest fears or loftiest dreams and know that he is not going to betray your confidence. Whether in personal relationships or in his practice, he is a trustworthy sounding board and a friend who will not just listen to you but will also hear you.

"He has a great sense of humor. He's funny as heck. He always tells the corniest jokes. He was sitting in my office one day and asked me, 'Who is the patron saint of emails? St. Francis of Assisi (cc).' And that's the kind of stuff you will get from him, but underneath it all is a very real, very caring person. Last year, I went through a divorce and had to change all my estate paperwork. I made him my trustee. He's the acting trustee of the trust until my children are forty, and then it reverts back to them. That's how much I trust him. I would say the thing that sets him apart from most advisors is that he has a much deeper level of concern for doing the right thing by his clients. Some have the motto 'don't do harm,' and as long as they don't do harm, they feel good about what they do. His standard is much more about being the best and what he can do that is best for his clients.

"Scranton is very gifted intellectually. His approach is far more analytical, and that's where Anthony and I are different. Anthony is analytical like David. He wants his clients to understand what they are investing in and why. I think that's why Anthony became an attorney, so he could offer a full array of services.

"Anthony and I both come from a place of wanting to help people, and sometimes that means protecting them from themselves. I had a couple come in who wanted to take a $50,000 distribution from their IRA. I quickly ran a calculation on the taxes that they would have to pay because of the way Social Security taxes are structured. They thought they were only going to have to pay $5,000; but they discovered that they were going to have to pay $29,000. That stopped them in their tracks. When we can do something like that for people, that's a high for us. We want people to be successful in retirement.

"Those kinds of success stories really drive us. That's where Anthony and I are very much alike. When you can trust somebody to always do what's right, to always do what's in the other person's best interest—you can't get much better than that."

The Perspective of my Clients

I recently had two of my clients over to my home to meet with the publisher. She wanted to get an impression of what my clients felt about the service that I and the rest of my staff at Providence Financial provide. I called upon Linda Henrikson, an Emmy-winning costume designer in Hollywood who is retired. She was joined by her neighbor and friend Linda Beaird, a retired former executive with Anheuser-Busch. In our office, we affectionately refer to them as the "Two Lindas." Linda Henrikson became a client of mine in 2008.

When you can trust somebody to always do what's right, to always do what's in the other person's best interest— you can't get much better than that.

"How I got to know Anthony was a little strange," said Henrikson. "I received a letter from someone I didn't even know that recommended him. I had all my money in Bank of America. I had a girlfriend, years and years ago, who was a financial person with Merrill Lynch. She passed away, and the guy who took over from her quit, so I just moved my money over to Bank of America, where I had my checking account.

"I was working all the time and was totally remiss about paying attention to my money. Then one day, I get a statement saying that my account had suffered a loss of $50,000. Now I had seen losses of $1,000 before, even a couple of thousand. I didn't pay much attention to those because the market would bounce back; but $50,000 got my attention. Then a couple of days later, I get this letter about Anthony. I asked a friend of mine named Ron to go with me to meet Anthony. Ron was a producer and knew about money and financial things. We met Anthony at his office, and Ron asked him a bunch of questions.

"As we left his office, I felt that Anthony was so engaging and genuine, and I just sensed that he was so honest. And Ron told me,

'You move your money to him right now. He's a good guy.' So I did. That was the start of our relationship.

"When I retired, it was perfect. I knew how to make money. I just didn't know what to do with it. The first few months into retirement were a little daunting, because I was used to having a large amount of money coming in every week. Now I had to learn how to live on a budget. And once I realized that Anthony had structured my investments so that I wasn't going to have to worry about money anymore, life got much better."

Linda Beaird retired when the company she worked for was bought out in 2010. Her stock options were a substantial financial windfall. She is Linda Henrikson's next-door neighbor and best friend. When she and her husband were talking about what to do with their money, Henrikson suggested they give me a call.

"I worked at Anheuser-Busch for years," said Beaird. "When they decided to sell in 2008, I still had a 401(k) and a ton of Anheuser-Busch stock. They finally settled the merger in 2010, and I sold my stock for eighty dollars per share. Now I was sitting with all this cash, and I called a big firm in New York. The guy I spoke with on the phone sent me some forms and did a risk assessment with me, but the only service I got was when I would call him. I was talking with Linda [Henrikson] about it, and she told me about Anthony.

"What impressed me about him was that he took the time to educate me on the different investment options. We met three different times for about an hour each time, and he had a chalkboard on the wall and was my teacher about investing before I ever became a client. He didn't mind me asking all the questions I needed to ask. And I really felt good about knowing what I was doing at the end of that third session.

"I moved my money over to Anthony, and I felt comfortable talking with him about all of my financial affairs. Then when my

MORE LIFE THAN MONEY

husband passed away, his office sent condolences and called to check on me. Now I feel comfortable knowing that I can call Anthony's office anytime, and I always get the information I need. I can ask questions and get answers right away. I trust that he is going to tell me the best advice for me, not just what I want to hear."

"Trust was a huge issue with me," Henrikson said. "Not only trust, but there's a moral fiber in that company that you can't find anywhere else today. That's the first thing I tell everybody about him. This man is so morally straight that you don't have to worry about your money. He would no more cheat anybody than the man in the moon. You feel safe with him handling your financial concerns."

"That was one of the reasons I went with Anthony," said Beaird. "Back when I started, I spoke with several people. I went to my credit union, and they had an advisor who wanted to talk to me only about annuities. That's all he knew. I didn't want to just do that. I wanted to be a little more diversified. I now have two annuities and I like them; but that's just a part of it. It's not the whole thing."

"Anthony talks about your life and helps you put the pieces together," said Henrikson. "During my career, I was responsible for multimillion-dollar budgets; but when it came to my personal finances, the only thing I was confident about financially was how to put my paycheck into the bank. That's about it.

"When you retire, you realize that your earning potential has stopped, and that's scary. He helped me resolve that fear. I had a financial planner in Bank of America before Anthony, and he was very good about staying in touch with me. Then he got moved up the ladder, and my account got turned over to a guy I didn't know. The guy never called me. I should have picked up the ball, but I was working eighteen-hour days. When I got my statement that showed a $50,000 loss in my account due to the 2008 market collapse, I thought to myself, isn't it the financial planner's job to call you when the market starts going down?"

"I grew up in a family that was much different from Linda [Henrikson's]," said Beaird. "Linda's family had money. My family did not. My father and mother had four kids, and they went through some really hard times where they couldn't do what they wanted to do. After my mother died, I took over my father's finances and refinanced his house so he could reduce his monthly expenses. He had only $2,000 a month coming in. That's not a lot of money. I didn't ever want to be in that situation and not in control.

"Anthony has educated me so that I feel like I not only have control of my money but I know what I am doing with my money. When potential clients ask Anthony for references, he will have them call me. I can talk with them for a half hour about everything that he has done for me as my financial advisor. I encourage them to talk with Anthony and have him do a risk assessment with them. When you're younger, you can handle more risk than when you're older. If you lose some money when you're young, you know you have time to earn it back and recover from the loss. When you're older, you don't have the time to recover the loss.

"The most important thing is that they are comfortable with Anthony. When he and I talked, he wasn't just trying to direct me toward one particular investment that he was pushing. We went through stocks, bonds, mutual funds, income, the whole routine, and I was very comfortable knowing that my money was going to be well placed in the types of investments that were best for my goals and my risk tolerance. That's the difference between Providence Financial and other advisors."

"I sum up my experience with Providence Financial in five words," added Henrikson. "Honesty. Integrity. Family. Kindness. Faith."

The Better Way To Retire

The emerging trend in financial advising is that many brokers are leaving the national brokerage and Wall Street firms and starting to go independent. There are more independents today than ever, and I think that's going to be a growing trend. The challenge with that, though, is that most of the independent advisors have been indoctrinated into the Wall Street philosophy. I personally think it is a cancerous philosophy that does not serve the best interest of the client. When you interview someone to be your financial advisor, ask the hard questions about how they are going to preserve your principal and protect your retirement.

David Scranton is the founder of Advisors' Academy and has been my personal mentor for over a dozen years. There are some people in this profession that are smart. He is a genius. David was in the world of Wall Street for years, and in 1998, he started realizing that a major correction was coming in the stock market. By 2000, the market had gone up sixteen- or seventeen-fold, and he knew that it wasn't going to last. Because of this conviction, he walked away from Wall Street, and he wound up taking all his clients with him. He started his own firm and recommended that his clients get out of the Wall Street investment philosophy, because he knew that it was the right thing to do. His book, *The Retirement Income Stor-E!*, tells his story and goes into greater detail on the investing for income philosophy. I highly recommend it.

In 2006, David founded Advisors' Academy, bringing together independent advisors from across the country, all of whom operate with the guiding principle of doing what is best for their clients. Advisors' Academy is a large brain trust where we get together and share what's going on in the industry, collaborating on research and brainstorming to find a better way in every financial situation.

There was a point in history when people believed the world was flat. No matter what you told anybody, the world was flat—until someone proved that the world was round. It's the same thing today in the investment paradigm. Everybody believes you just have to sell shares as long as you only sell 4 percent of your portfolio each year. The problem is that people are living longer today than ever before. Fifty years ago, the average life expectancy was sixty-seven. If you retired at sixty and died at sixty-seven, then selling shares for five or ten years or less was fine, but if you live to be a hundred, you wouldn't have a very good retirement. Today, people are living longer in retirement than they did when they were working, and the chance of living until one hundred is much greater. You cannot go into retirement selling shares, no matter how little it is, and you should be able to count on your income until you no longer need it.

It is my sincere hope and prayer that I have helped you sort out the puzzle pieces in your life and that you now have a clearer picture of what your retirement can and should look like.

If you are in the Los Angeles metropolitan area, call us or come by and see us:

Providence Financial & Insurance Services
20335 Ventura Boulevard, Suite 125
Phone: (818) 887-6443

I leave you with this quote from Dave Ramsey: "I believe that through knowledge and discipline, financial peace is possible for all of us."

COVID-19: How a Virus Changed the World

IN A BOOK ABOUT FINANCES, it would be remiss of me not to share some thoughts on COVID-19 and the impact it may have on your retirement. The main theme of this book is, "What you don't know *can* hurt you." COVID's impact on the economy and the stock market is an outcome we simply can't know. From a macro viewpoint, we can't know the long-term effects on the world's economy. From a micro viewpoint, we can't know the long-term effects on your retirement. The best-case scenario is that the vaccines prove to be effective, the economy remains open, and the stock market continues to march forward.

The worst-case scenario would be the opposite.

Because there are equally good arguments to support both possibilities, many investors are in a quandary and don't know what to do. My suggestion is to prepare for the worst-case scenario. If you don't prepare for the worst-case scenario and it occurs, you risk losing a good chunk of your retirement. If you're already retired, this may mean having to cut back on your lifestyle. If you're not retired yet, you may have to keep working for another few years. But if you've prepared properly, and the worst-case scenario becomes reality, you should be just fine.

We're all hoping the virus gets extinguished (or is at least under control), everyone gets back to work, and stocks continue their upward march. However, we should spend some time discussing the worst-case scenario so you know how to prepare for it.

The facts regarding COVID-19 are changing so fast that any conclusions that make sense at the time of this writing in late 2021 may be debunked by the time you read it. Let's examine the facts as we know them today and discuss the possible conclusions.

The Initial Economic Impact

During the initial stage, COVID-19 caused the world's economy to come to a screeching halt for two reasons. First, many businesses had to close due to governmental regulations. Second, people weren't spending for fear of the unknown future of their finances. As a result, this virus truly created an economic stoppage.

The restaurant industry was the first and hardest to get hit. According to Sean Kennedy, executive vice president of public affairs for the National Restaurant Association, "Restaurants are a $2.5 trillion driver for this economy, employing one out of every ten workers."[31] Furthermore, 70 percent of operators laid off their work force, and the restaurant industry laid off three million workers.

---

31   Denver ABC 7, TheDenverChannel.com, "3% of US Restaurants Have Permanently Closed Due to COVID-19 Pandemic, Experts Say," https://www.thedenverchannel.com/news/national/coronavirus/3-of-us-restaurants-have-permanently-closed-due-to-covid-19-pandemic-experts-say.

Because people were afraid to get on airplanes, travel and tourism were also hit hard. As of May 2020, seven out of ten hotel rooms were empty across the United States.

Early on, hotels had lost $46 billion in revenue.[32] Nearly 50 percent of the direct hotel workers were laid off or furloughed,[33] which translated into a loss of $1.7 billion of income per week for these workers. With an occupancy rate of 35 percent or less, COVID-19 caused thirty-three thousand small businesses in the hotel industry alone to be at risk. [34]

The airline industry was in trouble as twenty-six thousand passenger aircraft were grounded, causing some twenty-five million jobs to be at risk, according to *Time*.[35] In June 2020, the International Air Transport Association (IATA) had warned that carriers could lose more than $84 billion in 2020,[36] and *Time* reported that most airlines would face bankruptcy in two to three months without government help.[37] Fortunately, the government provided roughly $40 billion of bailouts to keep the industry afloat. As of early 2021, CNBC reported

32   TRUiC Startup Savant, "The Hotel Industry Has Lost $46 Billion—and Counting," https://startupsavant.com/news/hotel-industry-lost-billions.

33   CNBC, "Hardest Hit Industries: Nearly Half the Leisure and Hospitality Jobs Were Lost in April," https://www.cnbc.com/2020/05/08/these-industries-suffered-the-biggest-job-losses-in-april-2020.html.

34   *Forbes*, "Hotel Industry Faces Huge Crisis in Coming Months, Discusses Recovery Solutions," https://www.forbes.com/sites/lealane/2020/03/18/hotel-industry-faces-huge-crisis-in-coming-months-discusses-recovery-solutions/?sh=4167e8b9e93c.

35   *Time*, "Two-Thirds of the World's Passenger Jets Are Grounded Amid COVID-19 Pandemic. Here's What That Means," https://time.com/5823395/grounded-planes-coronavirus-storage/.

36   IATA, "Industry Losses to Top $84 Billion in 2020," https://www.iata.org/en/pressroom/pr/2020-06-09-01/.

37   *Time*, "Coronavirus Will Bankrupt Most Airlines by May Without Government Help, Analyst Warns," https://time.com/5803757/coronavirus-airlines-bankrupt/.

that the actual losses for 2020 were only $35 billion,[38] which, although much less than had been predicted six months earlier, is still a huge number. It is going to take years for the travel industry to recoup these losses and get back to prepandemic levels.

The manufacturing industry, which employs some thirteen million workers, was hit hard because many of the jobs are on site and could not be carried out remotely. There was also a reduced demand for industrial products around the globe. "Slowed economic activity" is a nice way of saying no one was spending any money. As of August 2020, the manufacturing industry had lost 750,000 jobs during the previous six months. Scott Paul, President of Alliance for American Manufacturing, pointed out that these hundreds of thousands of factory layoffs "are becoming permanent rather than temporary."[39]

As a result, many companies have already filed for either Chapter 11 or Chapter 7 bankruptcy. Chapter 11 bankruptcy allows a company to restructure its debt, whereas Chapter 7 bankruptcy indicates that the filer is throwing in the towel. Here is a short list of some companies that have already filed for one type of bankruptcy or another: Aldo Group, CMX Cinemas, Frontier Communications, Gold's Gym, Hertz, JCPenney, J.Crew, Neiman Marcus, RavnAir, Speedcast International, Sur La Table, Tailored Brands, Religion, and Virgin Australia. This is only part of the story. Because of COVID, one million small business have been shut down.[40]

---

38 CNBC, "U.S. Airlines' 2020 Losses Expected to Top $35 Billion as Pandemic Threatens Another Difficult Year," https://www.cnbc.com/2021/01/01/us-airline-2-losses-expected-to-top-35-billion-in-dismal-2020-from-pandemic.html.

39 Alliance for American Manufacturing, "Manufacturing Adds 26,000 Jobs in Latest Employment Report," https://www.americanmanufacturing.org/blog/manufacturing-adds-26000-jobs-in-latest-employment-report/.

40 Wall Street Journal, "COVID-19 Shuttered More than 1 Million Small Businesses. Here Is How Five Survived," https://www.wsj.com/articles/covid-19-shuttered-more-than-1-million-small-businesses-here-is-how-five-survived-11596254424.

We can't know what the final outcome will be until after this pandemic is under control. One expert witness, the International Monetary Fund (IMF), testifies that the economy will likely suffer the worst downturn since the Great Depression.[41] These bankruptcies illustrate the suffering that COVID-19 has already inflicted on world economics. All of this economic devastation is not going to fix itself overnight, regardless of what we're being told. The rest of this section is a foretaste of what the world's economy *could* be in the coming months (and likely years) and what you can do to prepare yourself.

The Future Economic Impact

The breadth and depth of the aftermath of the coronavirus will depend on how effective the vaccines prove to be and how quickly economic spending gets back to its prepandemic levels. The vaccines appear to be working and certainly give us a reason to be positive. As of mid-2021, cases started to decline, and states have mostly opened up again.

Will this trend continue? As of this writing, there are rumors that the economy may once again have to be shut down due to the new Omicron variant virus that is on the rise. On a more positive note, the world's governments have done everything in their power to fix this economic crisis; they've pulled out every arrow in their quiver and have unleashed a fury of quantitative easing (printing money) with the apparent intent of continuing to do so as long as necessary.

Under former president Trump, the United States spent $3.5 trillion to keep the economy from going into the toilet. This is a huge number that exceeds the entire gross domestic product (GDP)

---

41   *The New York Times*, "I.M.F. Predicts Worst Downturn Since the Great Depression," April 14, 2020, https://www.nytimes.com/2020/04/14/us/politics/coronavirus-economy-recession-depression.html.

of many of the world's largest economies, like Italy, Brazil, and even Canada. As a matter of fact, only six other countries have GDPs that are larger than the amount that the United States has spent so far fighting this virus! Furthermore, President Biden added another $1.9 trillion of stimulus,[42] and there is another $3.5 trillion "infrastructure" package on the table.[43]

Will all this stimulus solve the long-term effects of this pandemic and the ensuing economic turmoil, or are the government's tools simply a short-term Band-Aid? There are valid arguments on both sides, but this is something else that we just can't know for sure. Because of these stimulus payments and the added liabilities, US debt skyrocketed to 136 percent GDP, which means that the government owes a lot more money than it takes in each year. As of the second quarter of 2020, the GDP for the United States was $19.5 trillion, and the national debt was approximately $26.6 trillion, which leaves a deficit of $7.1 trillion. When you divide the $26.6 trillion deficit by the $19.5 trillion GDP, you have a debt-to-GDP ratio of approximately 136 percent.[44]

These numbers are big ... really big ... and unfathomable to most people, so let's bring it down to Earth and use an example that may be closer to home, in case you're having a difficult time wrapping your head around all of the zeros. Let's say that you make $100,000 per

42   CNBC, "Biden Signs $1.9 Trillion COVID Relief Bill, Clearing Way for Stimulus Checks, Vaccine Aid," https://www.cnbc.com/2021/03/11/biden-1point9-trillion-covid-relief-package-thursday-afternoon.html.

43   CNBC, "Democrats' $3.5 Trillion Budget Package Funds Family Programs, Clean Energy and Medicare Expansion," https://www.cnbc.com/2021/07/14/democrats-3point5-trillion-budget-package-funds-family-programs-clean-energy-medicare-expansion.html.

44   Federal Reserve Bank of St. Louis, "Debt to GDP Ratio: How High Is Too High? It Depends," https://www.stlouisfed.org/open-vault/2020/october/debt-gdp-ratio-how-high-too-high-it-depends.

year, and you use this to pay your bills and support your lifestyle. But let's also throw in the stark reality that you owe $136,000 on credit cards; you would have a debt-to-income ratio of 136 percent, the same as the US government's. How are you going to pay those credit cards off? If you're already spending your entire $100,000 of revenue to pay your bills and fund your lifestyle, where are you going to get the difference from? First, you can go through all your expenses to see if you are wasting any money on things you've been paying for but no longer use or need.

Second, you can increase your income, maybe sell some things, have a garage sale, get rid of that extra car, or get another job. You can reduce your spending, cut back on your lifestyle, or take fewer vacations. Whatever you decide to do, there's no arguing that it's going to take a long time for you to pay off this debt.

The government has these same options at its disposal. First, the government can audit its various agencies and find ways to cut waste by reducing expenses or eliminating nonproductive programs.

It can increase its income by establishing economic policies that would allow businesses to flourish and increase employment. Another way that the government can increase its income is by raising taxes. The Tax Cuts and Jobs Act, which became law in 2017, sunsets in 2025, and many of the tax breaks that were put into place will expire. Plus, Biden is lobbying for tax increases. Finally, the government can reduce spending, which may require it to cut benefits, including things like Medicare, Social Security, and other general welfare programs.

Now, let's go back to your example: you currently make $100,000 per year and owe $136,000 on credit cards. But it gets worse—you lose your job. How are you going to pay your credit cards off now? Is this even a realistic possibility? On the contrary, you may have to spend even more on those credit cards and increase your debt just to survive! Obviously, it's not the panoramic view of the American dream you pictured when you planned out your retirement. Unfortunately, this is the very predicament the government finds itself in. With over a million small businesses no longer operating and nearly twice as many unemployed workers as there were prepandemic, the government has just had a massive decrease in tax revenue.

Businesses that are closed aren't going to pay taxes, and the IRS is going to have a hard time collecting from all those workers without jobs. The government has been forced to add to its debt as they install stimulus package after stimulus package to keep the economy afloat.

The good news is that vaccines have become readily available. If they prove effective over the long run, and we can continue to live a somewhat normal life, consumers will likely keep spending their money. However, there are still a lot of things we can't know. Is it possible that the vaccines are not as effective as we were hoping for? Will consumers resume their spending habits like they did before? Will there be additional mutant viruses that prove to be even more contagious than the original virus?

What about the stock market? How has it been affected by all of this, and what can we expect for the future? If you're invested in stocks or mutual funds, you better have an opinion about this, because your conclusion may affect your retirement or whether you can retire when you've been planning.

Ray Dalio, who runs the world's largest hedge fund, Bridgewater Associates, sees the coming economic downturn as resembling the effects of the Great Depression, which lasted from 1929 to 1933 and is regarded as the worst economic crisis in American history.[45] The

---

45   CNBC, "Ray Dalio Predicts a Coronavirus Depression: 'This Is Bigger than What Happened in 2008,'" https://www.cnbc.com/2020/04/09/ray-dalio-predicts-corona-virus-depression-this-is-bigger-than-2008.html.

Great Depression saw US unemployment hit a peak of nearly 25 percent, while gross domestic product declined by nearly 30 percent. Will these dire predictions come true? We don't know, but this is what some experts are predicting.

A lot of experts, though, point out that there are some significant differences between the Great Depression and our current situation. First, the Great Depression was preceded by a massive boom in the economy, the Roaring Twenties, and booms are almost always followed by busts. During the last thirteen years since the 2008 recession, our economy has not necessarily been booming, but rather has been growing at a steady and, some would argue, even slow pace.

Second, the Federal Reserve's decision-making structure during the Depression was decentralized and often ineffective.

Finally, and I believe most substantially, our current crisis has been met with an economic response like no other. The Fed has pumped trillions of dollars into the economy and is committed to thwarting any resemblance of another Depression-like scenario.

There is a saying, "Don't fight the Fed," and I believe that the stock market's response to all the stimulus is the perfect proof that there is some truth to this. The Federal Reserve has bailed out businesses and workers alike, and the stock market has had a strong V-shaped recovery as a result.

Does this mean we are out of the woods? Not necessarily. The market has skyrocketed above the levels that it had previously reached in February 2020, but the fundamentals are significantly different. Pre-COVID, unemployment was only 3.8 percent, but as of the first quarter of 2021, it had ballooned to 6.7 percent. GDP for 2019 grew by 2.3 percent, whereas in 2020, it contracted by 3.5 percent. Pre-COVID, the government was only $22.8 trillion in debt, but as of mid-2021, the government's debt is rapidly approaching $30 trillion,[46] an increase of over 27 percent in just the last eighteen months!

When analyzing the before and after of the economy and the stock market, it is very apparent that there is a massive disconnect between the fundamentals of today and where the stock market stands. In case this is not evident, though, just browse the headlines. The *Wall Street Journal* has one that reads, "When the Stock Market and Economy Seem Disconnected."[47] A *Forbes* headline reads, "The Disconnect Between Stock Performance and the Economy: 4 Reasons Stocks Are Poised to Fall."[48] Finally, a CNBC headline states, "The U.S. Is in a Recession, but the Stock Market Marches Higher. Here's Why There's a Disconnect."[49] And the list goes on and on. The question then is not whether there is a disconnect but why.

There are several plausible reasons. The markets are forward looking, and if things look like they're getting better, the markets are encouraged. Presently, the market is optimistic now that vaccines seem to be working and the unemployment rate has dropped.

Consumer spending has increased recently, which is yet another beneficial factor.

Many experts, though, including me, believe that the biggest reason why the market has not plummeted into Depression territory is because of the stimulus packages the government has installed and

46   US Debt Clock, https://www.usdebtclock.org/.

47   *Wall Street Journal*, "When the Economy and the Stock Market Seem Disconnected," https://www.wsj.com/articles/when-the-stock-market-and-economy-seem-disconnected-11598002220.

48   *Forbes*, "The Disconnect Between Stock Performance and the Economy: 4 Reasons Stocks Are Poised To Fall," https://www.forbes.com/sites/mikepatton/2020/07/23/the-disconnect-between-stock-performance-and-the-economy-4-reasons-stocks-are-poised-to-fall/?sh=7134785a6271.

49   CNBC, "The U.S. Is in a Recession but the Stock Market Marches Higher. Here's Why There's a Disconnect," https://www.cnbc.com/2020/06/03/understanding-the-huge-disconnect-between-the-stock-market-and-economy.html.

apparently will continue to provide. A *Fortune* article states that if the CARES Act had not been passed, evictions and poverty rates would have soared, municipalities across the country would have gone bankrupt, and the major averages would have collapsed.[50] David Rosenberg of MarketWatch writes, "The stock market no longer thinks it needs the economy if it has the Fed."[51] He also adds that "as long as the Federal Reserve keeps pumping monetary stimulus into the financial system, the financial markets can continue to ignore the awful state of the economy." Finally, CNN Business reports that there are two main reasons for the booming stock market: first is the unprecedented stimulus from the Federal Reserve, and the second is the fear of investors missing out on monster returns once the economy recovers.[52] Without the trillions of dollars of stimulus, many professionals don't believe the market would be anywhere near the level it is at now.

So, let's ask ourselves, Can the government continue printing money and going into debt to keep the economy afloat? I have asked this questions hundreds of times to my clients, radio show listeners, and many others, and the answer I always get is a resounding *"No!"* But some experts say it's possible.

In the nineties, American economist Warren Mosler developed a concept that has become known as Modern Monetary Theory

50 *Fortune,* "This Is What the Stock Market Would Look Like if the CARES Act Never Happened," https://fortune.com/2020/07/15/stock-market-sp-500-cares-act-impact-us-economy-coronavirus-stimulus-checks-unemployment-ppp-loans/.

51 MarketWatch, "'The Stock Market No Longer Thinks It Needs the Economy if It Has the Fed,' David Rosenberg Says," https://www.marketwatch.com/story/the-stock-market-no-longer-thinks-it-needs-the-economy-if-it-has-the-fed-david-rosenberg-says-11595429130.

52 CNN Business, "America Is in Turmoil and Stocks Are Booming. Is the Stock Market Broken?," https://www.cnn.com/2020/06/03/investing/stocks-market-dow-jones-riots-coronavirus/index.html.

(MMT).[53] This theory touts that sovereign governments that issue fiat currency (money that is not backed by anything) do not need to issue bonds because they can simply print money at will. MMT purports that debt is simply a means to insert money into the economy without getting it back in taxes. If the economy overheats, MMT strategies conclude that taxes are a tool to take money out of the economy to cool it down. The only limit the government has in its ability to print money is the availability of real resources, including workers, construction supplies, etc.

As noted in a *Wall Street Journal* article, Stephanie Kelton, a Stony Brook University professor and proponent of MMT, believes that governments do not need to worry about how much debt they incur for spending programs because, unlike households and businesses, governments can never run out of money.[54] The constraint upon the government is not the deficit but rather whether the borrowing and spending spurs inflation and disrupts economic activity. Through the years, this theory has gained traction, and political leaders like Alexandria Ocasio-Cortez and Bernie Sanders have jumped on board in promoting it.

However, MMT has a lot of opposition. Paul Krugman, a Nobel Prize–winning economist, has warned that the United States would see hyperinflation if it was put into practice and investors refused to buy US bonds. Michael Strain, a *Bloomberg* economic columnist, titled an article he wrote on January 17, 2019, "'Modern Monetary Theory' Is a Joke That's Not Funny."[55] Warren Buffett has declared that

---

53   Mosler Economics/Modern Monetary Theory, "About Warren," http://moslereconom-ics.com/warren-mosler-bio/.

54   *Wall Street Journal*, "Can the U.S. Afford Democrats' Bold Promises? Why One Economist Says Yes," https://www.wsj.com/articles/can-the-u-s-afford-democrats-bold-promises-why-one-economist-says-yes-11553961600.

55   AEI, "'Modern Monetary Theory' Is a Joke That's Not Funny," https://www.aei.org/op-eds/modern-monetary-theory-is-a-joke-thats-not-funny/.

"I'm not a fan of MMT—not at all"[56] and that if it was implemented as many Democrats would love to see, it would bring "spiraling" inflation.

As we've already discussed, when you analyze the economy and the stock market, it's impossible not to see that there is a disconnect the size of the Grand Canyon between them. Imagine the current economy on one side of the Grand Canyon, with its toes hanging over the edge, gazing at the stock market on the other side. Something has to connect these two though, right? Because the stock market and the fundamentals of an economy are twins—they're supposed to go hand in hand. When you study the fundamentals of our current economy and compare it to the record highs of the stock market, you'll observe that there is a big gulf between the two. When you look closer, though, you realize that something *has* actually filled in this chasm. You reach down and pick up a hundred-dollar bill. Then you pick up another one. Then it dawns on you—the canyon that is separating the economy from the stock market is actually filled in with hundred-dollar bills ... billions of them!

That's the connector! Trillions of dollars of the government's stimulus money have filled in the canyon that is separating economic reality and the stock market!

Can the government's money-printing machine continue to fill in this gap without future consequences? Is it true that as long as the government is willing to continue printing money, the stock market no longer needs to rely on fundamentals? Although MMT says it's possible, this is something else we can't know.

---

56 Bloomberg/Quint, "Warren Buffett Is No Fan of Modern
    Monetary Theory," https://www.bloombergquint.com/business/
    buffett-no-fan-of-modern-monetary-theory-with-its-danger-zones.

What You Can Do To Protect Yourself

Let's get to the nitty-gritty. What should you do to protect your retirement nest egg? How exactly do you prepare for the worst? I can't tell you that if you do such and such, things will work out. Or if you follow this formula, the aftermath of the virus won't affect you at all. It doesn't work that way. What I can tell you is that this is not a time to freeze up out of fear. Nor is it a time to be complacent, thinking that the Federal Reserve, Congress, or your advisor is going to fix it. No one cares more about your money than you do; that's the cold hard truth. You need to be vigilant with your investments and your strategy, staying in the driver's seat and taking the wheel more than ever before. In short, you need a plan. I'm going to suggest you plan for the worst-case scenario *for you*. Take some time to get educated about different investments and strategies that you can use to protect your wealth during this time. Knowledge is power, so you must take the time to get the knowledge. But what if you don't have the time or the desire? Then find an advisor who does. Find an advisor who is willing to take the time to teach you how to protect the assets that you've accumulated over your lifetime. It's going to be a miserable day if the worst-case scenario happens, and you can't retire on schedule because you didn't take the time to search for help and come up with a plan.

As I've mentioned previously, I'm a Jesus Christ follower. To me, it's not all about the money. It's about using the gifts that the Lord has blessed me with to help others protect what they've earned. Yes, I am a financial advisor and an estate planning attorney. But more than that, I'm an educator. I take the time to learn about my client's goals, their dreams, their fears, and then educate them so that they have the knowledge they need to make informed decisions. Every team needs a coach, but a coach can't play the game. Find a coach who knows how to help you and who is willing to educate you. Ask the tough questions, and if your advisor doesn't want to answer them or you feel like he or she is beating around the bush, maybe it's time to find a new coach. I beg you to take the time to get educated, because what you don't know *can* hurt you.

ACKNOWLEDGMENTS

This book has been a tremendous undertaking and I could not have done it without my wonderful team!

The following is a tribute to the team members at Providence Financial and Insurance Services Inc., the company I founded in 1999.

Krystal Soutar, New Accounts Manager, Office Manager: You have been the glue that has held our team together. Thank you for continuously making our new clients feel as special as they deserve to feel. Without you, I shudder to think of where Providence Financial would be today. Your friendship has truly meant a lot to me!

Denise Frias, Marketing Coordinator: You have worn multiple hats the entire time you have been a part of the Providence team and have worn them well. Because of you, our marketing events and my speaking engagements have gone flawlessly. Thank you for being a valuable member of the team!

Gerry Alcala, Client Relationship Manager: There is no one better than you when it comes to speaking with those who contact us to learn more about our services. You have the uncanny ability of juggling my calendar to make sure it is constantly filled so that my time is efficiently spent talking with prospective clients. This is a very difficult job and you perform it well!

Jacqueline Thomas, Client Service Coordinator: The only reason that Providence Financial continues to offer the world class client service that we are known for is because of you. You have a wonderful personality and the ability to make our clients continue to feel valued. It's not easy to drop whatever you're doing to take a call from a client with a question, but you do a phenomenal job at it!

Rebecca Kasper, Executive Assistant: There are a million things that I would rather not be doing and because of you, I don't have to. You consistently do what is necessary to make sure I can focus on my responsibilities and I appreciate all of the small things you do that collectively make up the big things. As the newest member of our team, I can already tell you are a superstar in the making!

Anca Saccaro, Social Media Coordinator: Because of you, our clients can stay in touch with our business. You send out our e-newsletters, post on all the social media platforms that we use to keep clients informed, distribute my radio show, podcast, all the media appearances I'm involved in, and send out my YouTube videos so clients get critical updates. On top of all that, you perform your most important job of being a wife and mother in a manner that makes me fall in love all over again with you every day! Without you, our business wouldn't be anywhere near where it has grown to. I truly am in love with you!

The following is a tribute to the team members at Anthony Saccaro Law, A Professional Legal Corporation.

Cheri Torres, Senior Paralegal: When I hired you, I had no idea you would end up being the backbone of Anthony Saccaro Law, but that is exactly what has happened. Acquiring a law firm is no easy feat and I could never have done it without your help and expertise. Your ability to stay focused on your tasks and run a law firm at the same time is unmatched. I look forward to growing with you for many years to come!

Lisa Pereau, Paralegal: As the newest member of Anthony Saccaro Law, you've done fantastic in growing into your position. As the first point of contact when someone calls our firm for the first time with a legal problem, you have the unique ability to put them at ease and let them know that we are there for them. This is truly a valuable skill and I'm looking forward to watching you continue to grow into your position!

GET IN TOUCH

PROVIDENCE FINANCIAL & INSURANCE SERVICES, INC., 20335 VENTURA BLVD., SUITE 125, WOODLAND HILLS, CALIFORNIA.

(800) 256-3513 TOLL FREE
(818) 887-6443 LOCAL

WWW.PROVIDENCEFINANCIALINC.COM

WWW.PROVIDENCEFINANCIALPODCAST.COM

Printed in the USA
CPSIA information can be obtained
at www.ICGtesting.com
CBHW020248170124
3461CB00009B/13/J